The Santa M...
Flagship of Columbus' Voyage of Discovery

we call the indigenous peoples of the Americas "Indians" and refer to the islands of the Caribbean as the "West Indies". On Christmas Eve, 1492, the Santa Maria drifted onto a reef off Hispaniola and sank. Columbus returned to Spain on the Nina. With three subsequent voyages, he established a permanent link between Europe and the Americas, an achievement that has earned this determined explorer a page of honour in the annals of maritime history.

Photography, Text & Design by
Franz J. Rosenbaum, ARPS

Published by
Parabola Company
1105 - 50 Prince Arthur Avenue
Toronto, Ontario
Canada   M5R 1B5

Trade Distribution by
Firefly Books Ltd.
3680 Victoria Park Avenue
Willowdale, Ontario
Canada   M2H 3K1

Separations, Printing
and Binding by
Friesen Corporation
Box 720, Altona, Manitoba
Canada   R0G 0B0

Paper: Garda Art Gloss–basis 25x38-200M

ISBN 0-9682838-0-2

PRINTED IN CANADA

SAILS

like the wings
of a soaring bird
riding the wind,

setting the spirit free
to chase an elusive dream,
to challenge the beckoning sea.

FOREWORD

The first day of racing in the 1986 Canadian Lightning Class trials for the Pan American Games was blustery. It was, after all, September, and this was Toronto's Humber Bay. It was blowing better than 20 knots when we rounded the leeward mark, came hard on the wind and hiked our three hides over the side. And there was Franz Rosenbaum, sailing his Shark SAGA. Working the tiller with his leg, he hung low over the coaming, camera to his eye. We bore down on him, sailing the boat as flat as we could, watching Franz cross our bow and safely ease SAGA to leeward.

For anyone who races on Lake Ontario, encountering Franz at work is a common occurrence. But there are many sailors the world over who share this experience. Ask the Japanese Grand Prix racers who looked overboard during one Clipper Cup series in Hawaii to find Franz close alongside, swimming more than a mile offshore with his camera in a watertight housing, pressing the shutter. Or the crew of FRENCH KISS at the 1987 America's Cup in Freemantle, Australia, for whom Franz was a prying eye in a helicopter.

Franz's persistence during the Lightning Trials produced a picture that now graces the wall of my living room. His aquatic resolve in Hawaii resulted in the striking frame you will find in the Clipper Cup section. His portrait of FRENCH KISS flying downwind in a gust of 35 knots earned him $1,000 in the "Kodachrome Cup", a challenge issued by Eastman Kodak to the worldwide fraternity of professional yachting photographers. Franz the local occurrence is also Franz the international phenomenon.

Camera technology has improved to a point that just about everyone, myself included, can get lucky with a sufficiently large supply of film and occasionally come up with a respectable image. As editor of Canadian Yachting, I have met a fair number of people who take pictures of boats. Yet, very few qualify as yachting photographers. Franz Rosenbaum is one of them, which is astounding, because he is self-taught and has not had any formal training in photography. His professionalism lies in the seemingly simple task of capturing a yacht on a frame of film. The fact that he has been a sailor for decades and knows his subject matter like few others gives him an advantage over many of his colleagues. Luck is removed from the process by anticipating the right moment to release the shutter rather than waste film. His tenacity and determination are remarkable; for three months he pursued the NONSUCH, until he was finally satisfied with the results of his efforts.

Franz intended this book as a tribute to the glory of sailing, but it also serves well as a testimony to his art. Enjoy them both.

Doug Hunter

THE VOYAGE CONTINUES

Early man found himself ill-equipped to cope with the liquid element. The process of evolution – a chain stretching from the first seaborn bacterial cells to homo sapiens – had cast him ashore. Early man was of the land.

He watched in awe as a storm-driven sea pounded at the fringe of his domain, impressed with its tremendous force. Intrigued, he contemplated a swell rise and fall gently at his feet when the storm abated. Roaring turmoil and silent calm – bold challenge and subtle temptation.

To meet this challenge man had to step off the land. And one day he did. He noticed that logs float. He learned to lash logs together to form a raft. He hollowed a log to make a dugout. Raft and dugout allowed him to prod river, lake and sheltered bay.

His confidence growing, man fashioned fibre mat and animal skin, attached them to an upright pole on his craft to catch the wind – and he sailed.

The starting point of this epic voyage is uncertain. Man learned to sail before he learned to write. He made history before he was able to chronicle it. But he was now a man of the sea. Obscure as his prehistoric achievements will remain, this nautical ancestor of ours helped to launch the barges of ancient Egypt, the plodding junks of mysterious China and the swift longships of scourging Vikings. He spurred Jason and his Argonauts in their search for the Golden Fleece and whispered into the ear of Sindbad the Sailor as he spun the yarn of his seven adventurous voyages.

To satisfy an irrepressible curiosity, our seafaring forebear expanded the confines of his narrow horizon in ever larger and safer vessels. Navigating by the stars, he boldly ventured beyond the theory that the earth was a flat disc. He sparked the spirit of great explorers like Columbus, Cabot, Da Gama, Magellan and Hudson. In sailing ships he was able to conquer the vast expanse of the great oceans, discover new continents, and leave behind the legacy of a comprehensive image of our world.

And he lives on in us as we put to sea in sturdy cruisers and sleek ocean racers or experience the enchantment of a secluded lake in a 12-foot dinghy.

THE NONSUCH

Sailing ships enabled man to shape the course of history. The epic voyage of the NONSUCH is just one notable example.

On June 3rd, 1668, the ketches EAGLET and NONSUCH sailed down the Thames, bound for the New World. Their objective was plain: to find a new route that would give England independent access to the beaver fur trade with Indian tribes of the Northern region. Beaver hats were the rage in Europe and this most lucrative business was virtually monopolized by French colonists along the St. Lawrence river.

After only a few days at sea, the two vessels encountered a storm. Badly damaged, the EAGLET was forced to turn back. The smaller NONSUCH, measuring a mere 50 feet from stem to stern and under command of Captain Zachary Gillam, had to continue on her own.

On August 1st, landfall was made off the north coast of Labrador. With many icebergs in sight, the NONSUCH entered Hudson Strait. Treacherous currents in the strait and the uncharted waters of Hudson Bay, strewn with islands and shoals, slowed progress considerably, as did fog, and later, the first snow. Finally, after four months at sea, the NONSUCH anchored in the estuary of a river at the southern end of James Bay. Here Captain Gillam and his crew built a wooden cabin for shelter against the rigours of a seemingly endless northern winter.

In the spring of 1669 the ship's company received visits from Indians eager to trade beaver skins for hatchets, needles and "wampum", the small white shell beads that were the accepted currency among Indian tribes of the north.

It was not until June that the ice loosened its hold on Hudson Bay. The NONSUCH weighed anchor and returned to England, laden to the plimsoll line with a cargo of valuable beaver fur.

Encouraged by the success of her voyage, the businessmen and courtiers who had financed the NONSUCH venture petitioned the King of England for a Royal Charter. On May 2nd, 1670, Charles II granted a charter to the "Governor and Company of Adventurers of England trading into Hudson's Bay". With Prince Rupert as Governor, they were pronounced the "True and Absolute Lourdes and Proprietors" of and given rights to "Sole Trade and Commerce" for an area of 1,486,000 square miles of land — or about 40 per cent of what is now Canada.

Thus the remarkable NONSUCH played a pivotal part in the establishment of the "Hudson's Bay Company". Spanning more than three hundred years the "Bay", as it is known today, remains the world's oldest continuous commercial enterprise and was a significant factor in Canada's economic development.

To honour the spirit and courage of the men who sailed the NONSUCH three centuries ago, the Hudson's Bay Company commissioned the construction of a full-scale replica. During her visit to Lake Ontario I sailed on the new NONSUCH one blustery afternoon in the spring of 1970 and was amazed at her diminutive size and spartan accommodations. With the breeze aft of the beam she moved along remarkably well. However, with square sails and not much of a keel, her windward performance was not very impressive. Pulling my foul weather jacket tighter against the chill that hung in the air, I couldn't help wondering how her crew must have felt as the little ship negotiated icebergs in latitudes much further north in the year of 1668.

The new NONSUCH on Lake Ontario, anno 1969 (opposite).

THE PRIDE OF BALTIMORE

Baltimore Clippers, sleek vessels of light displacement, low freeboard and a generous sail area supported by distinctively raked masts, were America's answer to attempts by the British fleet to stifle trade with the fledgling "nation of renegades" during the War of 1812. Superior speed enabled these schooners to outrun their heavily armed opponents and prove themselves very successful as blockade runners and privateers. After the war they earned notoriety by smuggling opium from the orient and participating in the profitable West African slave trade.

The PRIDE OF BALTIMORE, sailing off Rhode Island, is a replica of these swift clippers (above).

THE BEAGLE

The barque H.M.S. BEAGLE sailed from Plymouth in 1831, bound for the Pacific via dreaded Cape Horn, on a mission to chart the west coast of South America and nearby islands. For five years she served as the floating study of a young, unpaid British naturalist, Charles Darwin. His observations of flora and fauna in South America and the Galapagos Islands laid the foundation of a thesis that would earn him the wrath and ridicule of scientists, clerics and the general public of his day. In 1977, a BBC documentary series recognized the achievements of the great evolutionist, featuring a replica of the BEAGLE as she retraced Darwin's epic 20,000-mile voyage. Launched in Valencia, Spain as MARQUES in 1917, she later reverted to her original name and served as a tourist vessel and sail training ship.

The MARQUES on her way from Bermuda to Halifax in the 1984 Tall Ships Race (opposite).

THE CALIFORNIAN

She brings to mind an era when sailing ships plied coastal waters and crisscrossed vast oceans in pursuit of commerce. Relying on windpower the fore-topsail schooner CALIFORNIAN is still engaged in the traditional inter-island dry goods trade.

Close hauled and with square sails reefed, the CALIFORNIAN rushes along in a fresh South Pacific breeze (above).

THE UNICORN

The brig UNICORN, a typical Baltic Trader of the 18th century, was built in Sibbo, Finland. Measuring 136 feet overall and carrying 7,362 square feet of sail, she was acquired by the Unicorn Maritime Institute as a training vessel for Sea Scouts and for the promotion of the port of Tampa, Florida.

With a fair wind on her starboard quarter, the UNICORN reaches down Tampa Bay towards St. Petersburg (opposite).

THE BLUENOSE

At the turn of the century, a keen rivalry had sprung up between the fishing schooners of New England and Nova Scotia. Racing back to port from the once fabulously rich fishing grounds off Newfoundland the "Gloucestermen" of Massachusetts were usually faster. To spur the "Bluenoses", as the Canadians were known along the eastern seaboard, to a challenge of the New Englanders, a Nova Scotia newspaper donated a prize. The International Trophy was to be awarded to the fastest bona fide Grand Banks fishing schooner. The first contest, held in 1920, saw the Yankee schooner ESPERANTO defeat Canada's DELAWANA.

In 1921, a schooner, drawn by William S. Rue of Halifax, was launched in Lunenburg, Nova Scotia. Aptly named BLUENOSE, she defeated ELSIE, the undisputed star of New England's Gloucester fleet, that year. Bested only once by the new GERTRUDE L. THEBOUD in a competition sponsored by Sir Thomas Lipton in 1931, the BLUENOSE vindicated herself a year later by beating her formidable rival in their next contest for the International Trophy.

The final race was held in 1938. A now aging BLUENOSE kept her record untarnished by winning a hard fought three-out-of-five series against her worthy opponent THEBAUD, thus never relinquishing the trophy she had first garnered seventeen years earlier.

The Second World War put an end to fishing on the Grand Banks. In 1942, the idle schooner was sold to a West Indies trading company. Four years later the BLUENOSE met her final match. Driven onto a treacherous lee shore ledge off Haiti by a storm, her graceful hull was torn apart by relentless breakers.

To revive the memory of yesteryear's glory, a new BLUENOSE was built to the original drawings and launched in 1963. Serving as a goodwill ambassador for Nova Scotia, BLUENOSE II has visited ports on both coasts of North America, the Caribbean and the Great Lakes.

BLUENOSE II, sails piled high, closing in on her home port Halifax (opposite).

A rising sun outlines the powerful schooner's bow at Baddeck, Bras d'Or Lake, Nova Scotia (above).

WINDJAMMERS

With every inch of canvas straining from spars that reach high into the stormy sky, the square-rigger shoulders the gale with ease. Lee rails awash, cutwater slicing through crest after crest, she flies by Cape Hope, leaving the Indian Ocean in her creaming wake to challenge the Atlantic.

Her captain, legs firmly planted on the aft deck, looks astern, waiting for the Cape to be swallowed by the horizon. Ever since the windjammer slipped her lines in Shanghai harbour two months ago, he has driven the ship hard. His sights are set on the premium of 10 shillings per ton London merchants will pay for the first tea of the season. But a prize of £100 and the veneration that await her master are even stronger incentives.

Calculating the angle of wind and waves, he decides to "harden up". From his speaking trumpet orders thunder across the ship. Oilskinned crew fight their way forward along the heaving deck to ease off and haul in braces. As the windjammer slowly nudges closer to the wind, her bow dips into a trough and the foredeck crew is pelted by sheets of driving spray. The captain's scrutinizing eye watches yardarms pivot into position. When all sails are trimmed perfectly to the new course he dismisses the mate with a grunt of approval. Then he turns and walks aft to the massive wheel, cautions the helmsman to stay sharp and "make sure she keeps that white bone in her teeth". Night falls. Ignoring dinner, he sends the cabin boy below for a mug of strong, black coffee. Until the small hours of the morning he paces the deck, a restless, solitary figure. He feels her surging power as the square-rigger eagerly storms northwest, into the dark, toward the eastern bulge of South America and the equator. He listens to the plaintive windsong rising from tight weather shrouds, the low rumble of the seas rolling along her hull, the rhythmic creaking of her timbers that synchronizes with the rhythm of the ocean's eternal swell. The sounds of a ship in tune with nature's might, a symphony in her captain's ear. "By Jove, she could do it", he mutters, "with a little luck through the doldrums and a fresh breeze in the North Atlantic she could have a record run".

"She" could have been any one of a score of windjammers, sharp-lined vessels carrying a cloud of sail, that engaged in the "Tea Races" of the nineteenth century. In 1866, five of these swift tea clippers, the FIERY CROSS, ARIEL, TAEPING, TAITSING and SERICA weighed anchor in Foochow within three days of each other. Within three days of each other all five gained the London docks – after 15,000 miles of hard sailing. The ARIEL and the TAEPING had been in sight of each other in the China Sea before heading off on different tacks. Three months later, they met again off Land's End. All sails flying the ARIEL, under Captain Keay and the TAEPING, with Captain McKinnon in command, engaged in an incredible neck and neck race along the English Channel and through the Strait of Dover. From the clifftops, crowds cheered until their voices gave out as they witnessed the spectacular duel between two thoroughbreds of the sea, tearing past all other sailing vessels and steamers bound for London. Although the ARIEL had been leading by five minutes off Dungeness, the TAEPING, drawing less water, made the dock 20 minutes ahead of her opponent. With the outcome of the race so close, it was decided that their captains should share the coveted prize. The SERICA, however, could claim an even more impressive victory: the only one to complete that voyage in less than 100 days, she was the fastest.

Six years later the THERMOPYLAE, then reigning champion of the tea trade, accepted a direct challenge from a newcomer, the CUTTY SARK, to race from Shanghai to London. The CUTTY SARK was leading by 400 miles when a storm in the southern Indian Ocean swept away her rudder. Not conceding defeat, she struggled on with a jury-rigged rudder. She arrived in London only a week after THERMOPYLAE. This remarkable feat of seamanship would earn the CUTTY SARK a permanent berth in the National Maritime Museum at Greenwich, England.

American square-riggers equalled their British cousins' daring on the route from New York to San Francisco, down the Atlantic and up the Pacific, via Cape Horn. In the days of the California gold rush, goods from pickaxes to pianos found eager buyers. And the demand for passenger space was at its peak; fortune hunters were anxious to stake out their claims. A fast ship would yield her owner a handsome return on his investment. In 1851 the FLYING CLOUD made the run in 89 days and eight hours, a record which stood for almost ten years.

A windjammer was what her name implied; at her best under a full press of sails. Her master, idolized by the public for his nautical exploits, was generally possessed of a dual personality. In port he was the centre of attention at social affairs. Always ready to entertain guests with tales of his seafaring adventures, he was a charmer of ladies and the envy of male landlubbers. At sea this suave raconteur would turn into an autocrat who cared not to have his authority questioned by anyone aboard his ship. One story has it that, on a particularly wild rush toward the Horn, a green-faced passenger had the temerity to ask the captain when he would consider reducing canvas. Measuring the poor soul with a cold stare, he replied that if sails needed shortening on his vessel, the wind would do that for him. Moments later the main royal exploded with a bang loud enough to resurrect the dead. The captain turned to his passenger and said: "Hope you are satisfied now", before he ordered hands aloft to cut away the madly thrashing shreds of a sail that was torn beyond repair.

An authoritarian he might have been, the captain of a clipper ship. But years of service before the mast had made him an expert in a profession that would tolerate neither patronage nor incompetence. Frequently the relationship between master and crew – usually a motley mixture of old salts, green adventurers and derelicts, culled by "crimps" from waterfront taverns – was strained. Punishment for disobedience was prompt and severe. The call "all hands on deck" would yank the off-watch from their bunks with lightning speed when a gale demanded sails to be shortened. After a skysail had been hauled up to the yard, securing it required a dozen or more hands to hustle up the ratlines to a crosstree, traverse the yardarm some 200 feet above a wildly pitching deck along the footrope, roll up the flailing canvas and tie it to the top of the yard with gaskets. This was a daunting chore at best. But en route to San Francisco, beating around the Horn from east to west in a blinding snow storm, squarely into the most tremendous seas to be found on any ocean, working aloft was hazardous in the extreme. The erratic gyrations of a whipping spar or a wildly flogging sail could shake a man out of the rigging and send him plunging to his death in the icy waters. Even duty on deck was perilous. A 60-foot "graybeard" would climb aboard to hurl a wall of solid water across the deck with a force that could pry a sailor from the handrail and sweep him overboard. Rescue was impossible – to lower a lifeboat into these mountainous seas would have been suicidal.

Occasionally a ship never made it past the Horn. With most of her sails blown out after battling westerly gales for weeks, low on stores and an overworked crew at the point of mutiny, her captain could opt for the ignominious "back door". Wearing the ship, he'd have to run to San Francisco by way of the Cape of Good Hope and across the vast Indian and Pacific Oceans. This route, including a stopover to take on provisions, would add thousands of miles, delay the ship's arrival in California by several months and leave little, if any, profit. Few skippers were prepared to make that prudent decision. Reluctant to have their reputation as hard drivers suffer, most captains continued, counting on a favourable slant of the wind to carry the ship well to the west of Tierra del Fuego and into the open Pacific, while brutal mates kept a rebellious crew in check with truncheons. Often this gamble paid off. But reports of missing ships were a regular occurrence. Concealed by heavy snow squalls or impenetrable fog waited a treacherous lee shore. Once a vessel was caught on its jagged rocks there was no escape – relentless surf would pound the ill-fated victim to pieces, leaving no trace or survivor to tell of the tragedy. The Horn had claimed its due.

At journey's end, many a young foredeck hand vowed never to walk the heaving deck of a square-rigger again. But after a few weeks ashore, he would find his hands practising an intricate knot or his rigging knife whittling the sleek lines of a clipper hull from a piece of bark. Before long, he'd succumb to a yearning that was as irresistible as it was inexplicable. It would draw him toward the waterfront, duffle slung across his back, ready to put his mark on the muster roll for another turn before the mast. The thrill of adventure and danger beckoned. Beyond the far horizon waited the mysteries of a distant land. The call of the sea was strong.

The square-riggers of today no longer carry tea from China or dry goods to San Francisco. Sailing under the flags of two dozen nations they are training ships for sea cadets, floating classrooms that familiarize aspiring mariners with the multitude of duties of the seafarer's trade – from coiling a line to steering the ship. Some of the work is menial: scrubbing the deck, galley duty, polishing brass, scraping rust or wielding a paint brush. Keeping a windjammer "Bristol fashion" is a never ending chore. Other tasks like climbing aloft to hand a sail are dangerous and require conquering an innate fear. It takes a few days to get rid of that squeamish feeling in the stomach and to grow sea legs. Soon the new cadets grasp the meaning of "heave ho" and before long they realize that only teamwork will keep the ship on her course. Subjugating their individual egos, they learn to rely on each other, become a crew. The first fresh breeze teaches respect for the forces of nature and the need to hang on. The time-honoured axiom "one hand for the ship and one for yourself" is still the primary rule. The spray sweeping across the foredeck stings just as hard as it did a hundred years ago and the pitching deck appears just as small from the topgallant now as it did then.

After a few months at sea the ship docks at a foreign port. Wearing smart shore leave uniforms, the cadets file down the gangway. The firm ground feels strangely unsteady. Ready to explore the wonders of a new country, they amble into town like old salts.

A few days in port and the ship sails again. A course is shaped to a new destination on another continent. And the learning continues: navigation and meteorology, standing watch, a turn at the wheel, mending a torn sail, splicing a brace, tying a knot until it can be done with eyes closed. And the endless scrubbing, polishing and painting as the ship sails on – day after day, night after night. Tough ropes make hands callous, sun and wind bronze the skin. During the off-watch there is time for swapping stories, friendly banter, a shanty or gazing at unfamiliar constellations rising in the night sky at different latitudes. There are more ports in exotic lands. But first and foremost there is the ship.

After a year or so the familiar landmarks of home appear in the distance. When the cadets step ashore, they do so with a new-found confidence. Some will become professional mariners. Others choose to pursue a career on land. All can claim to have sailed before the mast of a square-rigger, an experience they will draw from for the rest of their lives.

They are the "Tall Ships". Occasionally a fleet assembles to race across an ocean, to a city ready to greet the friendly invasion with open hearts. Even in port, these slender giants are an impressive sight. Landlubbers flock to the docks by the thousands to marvel at the towering forest of masts, the imposing size of hulls and the spotless order of it all.

They are ambassadors of international goodwill, these Tall Ships, and witnesses to a past known as the "Golden Age of Sailing".

A strong breeze puts her lee rail down as the EAGLE, every stitch of canvas set and drawing, drives headlong into North Atlantic combers. The combination of square sails on fore- and mainmast, but a fore and aft spanker and gaff-topsail on the mizzenmast designate the 295-foot long EAGLE a barque. Launched in Germany in 1936, she saw duty as a cargo carrier during World War II. Since 1946 she has served as the US Coast Guard's sail training vessel. Carrying 21,350 square feet of canvas, the EAGLE accommodates 19 officers, 16 crew and 180 cadets (opposite).

The DAR MLODZIEZY of the Polish Merchant Navy Academy was built at a Gdansk shipyard and launched in 1982. She is 310 feet long and has a complement of 17 officers, 20 crew and 130 trainees. As a full rigged ship the DAR MLODZIEZY carries square sails on all three of her masts. En route from the Canary Islands to Bermuda, the yard of her mizzen skysail was bent in a squall, preventing her from flying that sail in the 1984 Tall Ships race from Bermuda to Halifax, Nova Scotia (above).

Minutes after the start of the 1984 Tall Ships race from Sydney, Nova Scotia to Plymouth, England a heavy fog bank rolled in and gradually enshrouded the fleet. The 293-foot barque SAGRES of Portugal – on the left of the picture – and her younger sister of the same size, the German barque GEORG FOCK – on the right – are still in clear view. But the hull of Poland's DAR MLODZIEZY has already been swallowed by the fog and only her rig is barely visible (preceding pages).

The Russian four masted barque KRUZENSHTERN, owned by the Ministry of Fisheries in Moscow, established an early lead after the start at Sydney. This was to be expected because, with an overall length of 375 feet, she is the largest sail training ship afloat. She was built by J. C. Tecklenborg in Wesermünde, Germany and launched in 1926. Her 34 sails total 36,597 square feet. The skipper of the "downeaster" fishing smack I had chartered managed to track the giant down in this "pea soup" on his radar screen. But as I was taking her picture, three penetrating blasts of the KRUZEN-SHTERN's horn warned us that we were getting too close (opposite, top).

Three masted, but with square sails on the foremast only, the LEEUWIN is a barquentine. Launched in 1986 by the Tall Ship Foundation of Western Australia, the LEEUWIN provides high seas sail training for young Australians in the varied and often treacherous waters of the Pacific and Indian Oceans (opposite, bottom left).

SVANEN, a barquentine built in Denmark in 1922, was engaged in the Baltic trade for half a century before she found her way to Canada and was commissioned as a training ship for the Canadian Sea Cadets (opposite, bottom right).

As the wind picks up on a heaving North Atlantic, three cadets must face the tough task of securing the main topgallant high above the pitching deck of the Venezuelan barque SIMON BOLIVAR (above).

CLASS RACING

Also known as one-design racing, this is one of the most widely practiced forms of competitive sailing. One-design boats are identical in hull, rigging and sail area. This means that fitness and talent rather than a faster boat are the decisive factors for success.

Ranging from tiny dinghies to large keel boats, some classes enjoy tremendous popularity. Youngsters are usually introduced to sailing in the OPTIMIST, an eight foot pram. With over 300,000 built, this is the largest one-design class in the world. It is safe to say that, under the watchful eye of parent or instructor, most of tomorrow's Olympic medalists are learning about the caprices of wind and wave in an OPTIMIST today. A step up in size and almost as numerous is the 14-foot LASER, faster and physically more demanding. The largest class boat is the America's Cup Class yacht, which measures in at an overall length of 75 feet.

The number and variety of classes are immense. Some classes may be of regional or national significance only whereas others, like the colourful HOBIE catamarans and the J/24, enjoy worldwide popularity. But whether club regatta or world championship, wind and enthusiasm drive the fleet around the course. And the crack of a gun as the bow crosses the finish line is a sweet sound in the winner's ear.

The long and arduous road to the Olympics, the secret aspiration of many a young sailor, is paved with self-denial and sacrifice. Endless hours of practice, in weather fair or foul, hone sailing skills to a keen edge. Experimenting with rig tuning and sail shape should result in an increase in the always elusive "boat speed". Studying complex racing rules prepares for the split second decision that might mean a decisive advantage at a crowded starting line or mark rounding. There are years of long, exhausting trips to training camps and regattas, where coaches keep score. For only one boat in each of the Olympic classes is allowed to represent a country at the Games. Only the best earn the privilege to reach for Olympic Gold.

Youngsters generally get their first sailing experience in an OPTIMIST. The skill and spirit of these neophytes from 5 to 15 years of age is impressive as they compete for local, regional, national and even world championship honours in this tiny eight foot pram.

Competitors from as far away as Japan and Uruguay took part in the well-attended 1984 OPTIMIST World Championship on Lake Ontario (opposite, top).

A concept of Ian Bruce and designed by Bruce Kirby, the LASER was introduced at the 1970 "America's Teacup", a contest for new dinghies suitable for mass production. Champion Hans Fogh, who had also designed the sail, helmed the barely finished prototype to victory. Recognized by experienced sailors as a lightweight and affordable single-hander with excellent performance characteristics, the dinghy became an instant success. The LASER was introduced as an Olympic class boat at the 1996 Atlanta Games. LASERs from 58 countries competed, the largest number of national entries in any discipline at the Olympics.

With 94 sailors at the starting line for the 1980 LASER World's in Kingston, Ontario, participation was even stronger. Crowded mark roundings like this one were the order of the day (opposite, bottom).

In the catamaran family, HOBIE-18s are the favourites. Easily recognized by their colourful sails, these speedy multihulls make for exciting competition and are particularly popular in warmer latitudes. Nonetheless, a HOBIE-18 was the choice of Canadian adventurers Jeff MacInnis and Mike Beedell for a seemingly impossible task: to conquer the frigid waters and ice floes of the dreaded Northwest Passage in a small sailing craft.

Starting line of the HOBIE-18 World Championship 1987 in Humber Bay, Toronto (above).

Two veterans of the Olympics: the FINN has been sailed in eleven consecutive Olympic Games. At the helm of a FINN, 51 year old Paul Elvström demonstrated his talent to aspiring North American Olympians at a sailing seminar on Lake Couchiching, Ontario in 1979. Known as the "Great Dane", Elvström has won three of his four Olympic Gold Medals in the FINN and eleven World Championships in a variety of classes from dinghies to keelboats (opposite, top).

The FLYING DUTCHMAN was designed by Holland's U. van Essen as a two-handed dinghy with trapeze and spinnaker. Capable of planing in moderate winds, it is the fastest Olympic monohull (opposite, bottom).

The STAR, a two-handed keelboat, dates back to 1910 and had its Olympic debut in 1932. It was abandoned for a more modern design in the 1968 Olympics. But the STAR's popularity was strong; the old classic was re-instated at subsequent Olympic Games.

Start of the STAR fleet at the 1979 World Champoinship in Toronto, Ontario (above).

Prosaically called a 470 for its length of 470 centimeters, this lightweight two-hander with trapeze and spinnaker is very temperamental and requires split second reaction and agility to prevent capsizing. These characteristics make it the choice of the sport's daredevils. Introduced at the 1976 Olympics in Montreal, the 470 is the only Olympic boat that offers separate medals for male and female competitors.

470s jockeying for position at the start in Kingston, Ontario, where the sailing competitions were held (overleaf).

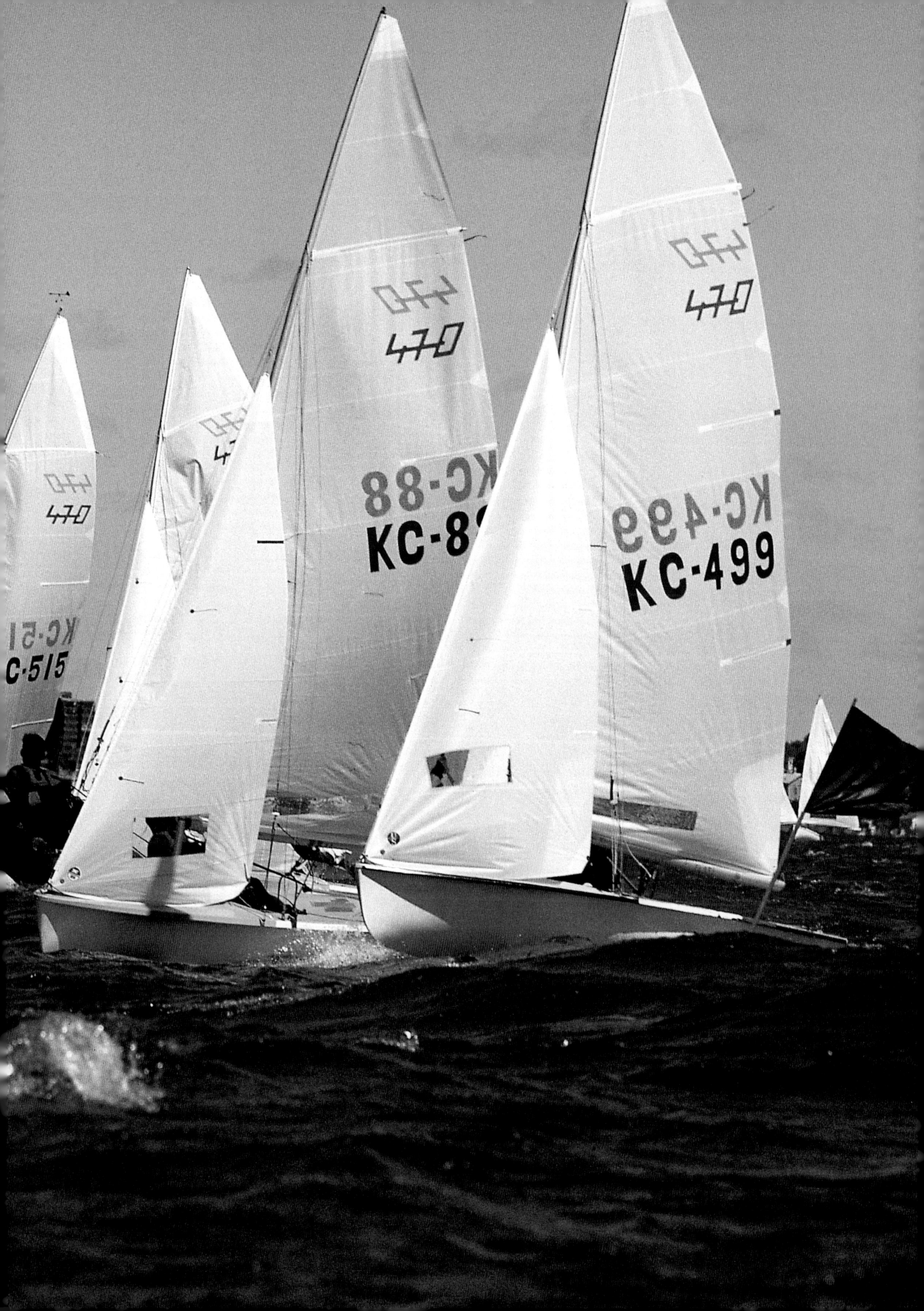

470
KC-88
KC-82
470
KC-499
KC-499
470
KC-51
C-515

The TORNADO is the thoroughbred of the Olympic classes. This two-man catamaran is capable of attaining a speed in excess of 20 knots in a good breeze. Under ideal sea conditions the TORNADO can actually exceed the speed of the prevailing wind, a perplexing, but proven fact (above).

Flying spray tossed up by the bow eclipses World Champion Hans Fogh as he and his crew push their SOLING hard to leave competitors in their wake (opposite).

The SOLING is the largest of the Olympic class boats. Requiring a crew of three, the SOLING was first sailed at the Munich Olympics in 1972. Since then it has attracted some of the most dedicated Olympic sailors.

SOLINGs reaching under spinnaker at the 1985 World Championship near Sarnia on Lake Huron (overleaf).

The J/24 is a prime example of a successful small keelboat. Strictly enforced class specifications prohibit any alterations that could give the boat an unfair advantage. This fact and the yacht's affordability account for the J/24's worldwide popularity.

Powered by a well-trimmed spinnaker, this J/24 slices through a wave (opposite).

The EIGHT METRE is a different approach to class racing. The International Eight Metre Rule, a mathematical equation to which the yacht must conform, permits a certain flexibility in design. But fair competition is assured because this rule produces boats very similar in appearance and performance. The designation "EIGHT METRE" is somewhat misleading inasmuch as it applies to one side of the rule equation; the average overall length of an EIGHT METRE is about 14 meters or 46 feet.

Three EIGHT METREs on a spinnaker reach at close quarters during the 1984 World Championship on Lake Ontario (above).

VISION, a wooden EIGHT METRE, was built in England in 1930. Restored and sailed by the Clarke family out of the Royal Canadian Yacht Club in Toronto, the black yacht is a remarkably fast competitor in spite of her age. She has had very sucessful campaigns in Europe and was a three time winner of the Sira Cup.

Sailing hard on the wind, VISION shows off the aesthetic lines of an EIGHT METRE yacht (overleaf).

GRAND PRIX OCEAN RACING

In 1905, eleven yachts of different sizes and rigging crossed the starting line at New York's Sandy Hook lightship in a race across the North Atlantic to the Cape Lizard lighthouse at the western entrance to the English Channel. Under command of Charlie Barr, a hard-driving skipper, who had successfully defended three America's Cups, the 187-foot American schooner ATLANTIC covered the distance of 3,013 nautical miles in 12 days, four hours and one minute. She garnered the "Ocean Cup", donated by German Emperor Wilhelm II. The smaller 163-foot German schooner HAMBURG took a respectable second place. She finished in 13 days, two hours and six minutes, beating the American 245-foot full rigged windjammer VALHALLA by more than 24 hours.

Numerous attempts to best the ATLANTIC's time, several by well prepared campaigns in modern yachts, simply failed. Hers was to be the longest standing record not only in yachting, but in the history of any sport. It was only in 1984 that a 60-foot catamaran succeeded in taking a few hours off the ATLANTIC's time. But multihulls have a definite speed advantage over monohulls and a monohull has yet to break the schooner's record.

As interest in offshore racing between yachts of different size, design and displacement increased, a handicap system to ensure a measure of fair competition became necessary. In 1923, the Cruising Club of America introduced the CCA rule. The first race under the RORC rule of the Royal Ocean Racing Club was held two years later. Unfortunately, the two systems were not compatible, as each tended to favour different design parameters. This caused a split between the Americans on one side and the British, other Europeans, as well as Australians and New Zealanders on the other. Although both factions were keen to compete against each other, it took almost five decades of arguments and concessions to agree on the International Offshore Rule in 1970. Appreciating that to formulate a rule which is equitable to different yachts in all weather conditions is as elusive as the quest for the Holy Grail, the IOR was as fair as a handicap rule could be. Subsequently, a number of other rules, bearing acronyms such as IMS, PHRF and MORC, were introduced. All have their strong points and weaknesses and challenge a yacht designer's talents. They encourage experimentation and improvement in boat building techniques and, by making use of new materials and sail cloth, contribute to the development of lighter, faster and sometimes, unfortunately, less seaworthy craft. All handicap rules have one aspect in common: by measuring the hull at predetermined stations and factoring in weight, sail area and other parameters, they determine a yacht's speed potential and calculate a handicap number that allows her to compete against yachts of different sizes and configurations.

A significant difference between class and handicap racing is the financial aspect. Whereas a dinghy or a small one-design keelboat is well within the means of any aspiring sailor, a state-of-the-art 45-foot yacht requires a substantial bank account. Designer's fees, construction, a full complement of sails and a battery of electronic instruments can easily exceed several hundred thousand dollars. This is comparatively reasonable in relation to a Maxi yacht of about 80 feet – the most powerful windship raced today – which can cost several million dollars by the time she is ready for competition. In return for his financial commitment, the owner hopes to gain a competitive edge. There are no guarantees, however. Some designs do not live up to expectations and never win a race. And even if successful, a new yacht cannot be expected to be a star performer for more that two or three seasons. Faster hull lines and more advanced technology will dethrone her sooner or later and send the resale value tumbling. Gone are the days of the sturdy but much heavier cruiser/racer with comfortable accommodations and a well-stocked galley. Sailed by the owner and his friends, a cruiser/racer would still fetch a reasonable price when she changed hands after years on the race course. The crew of a modern racing machine, culled from the ranks of Olympic veterans, sailmakers and specialists in onboard computer technology are experts, capable of driving the boat at her maximum potential from start to finish. They gobble down pre-cooked food, sleep in narrow pipe berths and are expected to be used as movable ballast. "Railbirding" means perching on the weather side, legs dangling outboard and being drenched constantly by flying spray. This keeps the yacht "on her feet", reducing heel as she beats to windward.

The five international events in which these modern yachts participate are known as the Grand Prix Circuit. Although similar inasmuch as they offer a combination of course, middle distance and long distance point-to-point races, each contest has a distinctively different flavour.

The Southern Ocean Racing Conference (SORC) was formed in 1961, when five yacht clubs in Florida and the Nassau Yacht Club in the Bahamas agreed to run this six race event. After the 138-mile Boca Grande race outside Tampa Bay, this series moves from St. Petersburg to Fort Lauderdale on the east coast of Florida with the 370-mile long distance race, a course that takes the fleet around Key West, the southernmost point of the United States. The 132-mile Ocean Triangle and the 40-mile Lipton Cup are sailed off Miami, followed by the 193-mile Miami-Nassau race. A final 35-mile triangle, hosted by the Nassau Yacht Club, can usually count on fine trade winds and a cloudless Bahamian sky. Four of the SORC races are sailed in the Gulf Stream, a mighty current flowing north through the Florida Straits. It tests the navigators' skill at any time. A strong northerly breeze blowing headlong into this current causes high and viciously steep seas, capable of dismasting a yacht or breaking her rudder post.

The SORC differs from the other four events of the Grand Prix Circuit in that it is raced annually and that the highest scoring individual yacht is the overall winner. The fleet is divided into five classes: from Class A for Maxi yachts to Class E for the smallest entries. A yacht is also awarded a prize for winning a race in her class, scoring an overall win in her class or winning a race overall.

The other four contests, held every two years, are team racing events in which national teams of three yachts compete against each other for top honours. The team accumulating the highest point total wins the Cup. However, some events also allow the participation of yachts that are not members of a team and the same fleet divisions as in the SORC are used. The long distance races of all events are open to any yacht that complies with the strict safety regulations of the International Yacht Racing Union.

Home base of the Sardinia Cup is Porto Cervo, the resort town on Sardinia's Costa Smeralda. Once a humble fishing village, it is now a town of magnificent villas, luxurious hotels and restaurants and the second residence of some of Europe's upper echelon. The Aga Khan, president of the Yacht Club Smeralda, was responsible for the promotion of Porto Cervo as a centre of major yacht racing events.

A well conducted public relations campaign brought a substantial international fleet to the Mediterranean island for the first Sardinia Cup in 1978. With 19 teams competing, participation reached its peak in 1982. The series, consisting of three triangles, a middle distance and a long distance race, is usually sailed in light to medium airs. But a Mistral can provide some heavy weather conditions, especially in the 300-mile long distance race, which starts at Porto Cervo, then leads through the Strait of Bonifacio between Sardinia and Corsica to Hyères in France and back to the finish at Porto Cervo.

"Down under", the Southern Cross Cup, organized by the Cruising Club of Australia, had its debut in 1967. Two 30-mile triangles off Sydney and the 180-mile offshore race can be expected to serve up some demanding conditions. Final event of this series is the popular Sydney-Hobart, an annual race dating back to 1945. Up to 200 yachts cross the starting line in Sydney harbour on Boxing Day. Gale force winds are common in Bass Strait between the southern tip of Australia and the island of Tasmania. After 630 miles of hard racing, weary sailors can look forward to a roaring welcome and a boisterous New Year's Eve party in the island's capital, Hobart.

Sunshine, billowing clouds and steady trade winds in the 20 to 25-knot range are the hallmark of Hawaii's Clipper Cup, first held in 1972 as the Around the State race. In 1978 the contest was extended to include three course races off Waikiki, for which Honolulu and the moutain ranges of Oahu serve as a picturesque backdrop, and a 150-mile middle distance race, which leads from Waikiki along the north shore of Molokai to Maui and back. The Around the State race, which concludes the Clipper Cup, circles the entire Hawaiian archipelago. Often encountering high winds in channels and calms in the lee of moutainous islands it can claim to be, at a total distance of 775 nautical miles, the longest course of the Grand Prix circuit.

Steeped in British yachting tradition, the Admiral's Cup is the oldest Grand Prix event and is, although not officially designated as such, considered the World Championship in offshore yacht racing. It is also, at least for non-English participants, the most perplexing. Starting from the Royal Yacht Squadron at Cowes on the Isle of Wight, three short races are sailed on the Solent, a narrow body of water between England's south coast and the Isle of Wight. Strong tides, counter currents, rocky shoals, mudbanks, oil tankers to and from Southampton, anchored freighters, ferries, hovercraft, hydrofoils and hundreds of pleasure boats of all sizes make the Solent a veritable steeplechase. Rather than setting marks, the race committee may select any of a total of 28 fixed buoys, which allows an almost infinite number of course configurations. Add to this weather conditions that can change rapidly from a lazy summer breeze to a 35-knot gale and the picture of what has always been considered the most prestigious Grand Prix event is complete. Collisions and hard groundings are frequent and few yachts manage to avoid the excellent repair facilities of Groves & Gutteridge at Cowes. At the press conference after one race in 1979, an American reporter remarked that the US team found the courses rather confusing. The jovial captain of the British team, the Honourable Edward Heath, ex-Prime Minister and an accomplished sailor, who had won the Sydney-Hobart race in 1969, pointed out that racing on the Solent in this manner was a tradition established many decades ago and that no changes were contemplated. He then ruefully added that the leading yacht of his own team had gone for the wrong buoy that very day and, as a consequence, the British squad had placed dismally. However, a few years later it was changed. When complaints of foreign competitors about the home team having an unfair advantage increased, two short course races were converted to Solent triangles and a third triangle was relocated to Christchurch Bay. The middle distance race starts in Cowes, crosses the English Channel to a buoy off Cherbourg in France and finishes at Gilkicker on the Solent. Like the Sydney-Hobart race, the Fastnet race is an annual fixture. First run in 1925, it is the oldest regularly held long distance contest and the final race of the Admiral's Cup. Starting at Cowes this 605-miler, fraught with changing winds and foul tides, follows the south coast of England to Land's End, rounds Fastnet Rock Lighthouse, off the southwestern tip of Ireland, and finishes at the port of Plymouth in Cornwall.

The recession of the late 1980's and the early 1990's has been responsible for a diminishing participation in Grand Prix racing. Most severely affected was the annual Southern Ocean Racing Conference. Entries in that series had dropped from 112 yachts in 1973, to 44 in 1988. The Board of Governors of the SORC tried various alternatives to revive this once popular annual event. Substituting shorter course races off Miami for the Ocean Triangle, the Miami-Nassau race and the Nassau Cup, the Circuit was compressed from a month into two weeks. But even this drastic measure did little to restore participation. Some of the old guard had tried hard to retain at least that traditional classic, the St. Petersburg-Fort Lauderdale long distance race but it, too, was finally abandoned in 1992, because of insufficient entries. The new format shortens the series to one week of tough around-the-buoys racing on three triangles of not more than a dozen miles each. One of the courses is just outside Miami's harbour entrance and the other two are located in sheltered Biscayne Bay. As a result, participation in 1996 reached an all time high of 155 boats; 95 entries were one-designs, complemented by 45 yachts racing under handicap rules and 15 multihulls. But the days when a substantial fleet, ranging from 80-foot Maxis to 30-foot Half-Tonners, raced six courses that covered almost 1,100 nautical miles in the open ocean now belong to the past. So do the social events hosted by the six hospitable yacht clubs along the route. These congenial gatherings were appropriate counterpoints for sailors arriving in port after the rigours of pushing their yachts to the limit. Having participated in two St. Petersburg-Fort Lauderdale races myself on a 30-footer, I can attest to the fact that, after a hot shower and a shave, shooting the breeze with the likes of Kilroy, Turner, Blackaller, North, Beilken or Cudmore and their crews was just as much part of yesteryear's SORC as was the competition on the water. Obviously, the new format is successful inasmuch as it has rekindled interest. However, without offering the challenges posed by long distance offshore races, the designation "Southern Ocean Racing Conference" is a misnomer.

It is not lack of interest or enthusiasm, but financial and time constraints that may bring about similar changes to the other Grand Prix contests.

TICONDEROGA

Harry E. Noyes, an industrialist of the American east coast, had no racing ambitions. His mind was set on some comfortable blue water cruising with family and friends when he commissioned Nathanael Green Herreshoff of Bristol, Rhode Island in 1935 to design a yacht for him to suit that purpose. Herreshoff obliged and TIGA, a 72-foot ketch, displaying a distinctive clipper bow and a graceful sheer, was launched in 1936. Her luxurious appointments included a large salon, generous staterooms, hot and cold running water and a well equipped galley with a refrigerator. Harry Noyes was rightfully proud of his stately vessel that would turn heads in every port. During the following years TIGA cruised extensively off New England and in the Caribbean.

All of the numerous racing yachts from "Nat" Herreshoff's drawing board, among them three America's Cup winners, had proven to be superior performers. That TIGA, the comfortable cruising yacht, was also a thoroughbred became obvious when friends persuaded Harry Noyes to enter her in the 1940 Miami-Nassau race. She affirmed herself to be fast beyond any expectation by setting a new record for the 176-mile course.

When her owner died in 1941, the US government requisitioned TIGA for the war effort. Her sleek white hull received a coat of grey paint and a machine gun was mounted on her deck. Able to hold her position under sail – without the use of a noisy engine – she was safe from detection by enemy sonar. This qualified her for duty as a submarine spotter and she was assigned a station off Boston.

After the war, TIGA was purchased by Allan P. Carlisle. Because her original name stayed with the Noyes family, she was re-christened TICONDEROGA. Her hull was restored to the traditional white and in 1947 she won the Marblehead-Halifax race, again setting a new record for that course of 366 miles.

In 1951 TICONDEROGA was sold to John Hertz Jr., who raced her to victory and a new record in the popular St. Petersburg-Havanna race the following year. This record still stands because all racing to Cuba was discontinued in 1960. Sailing from victory to victory, TICONDEROGA established new course records for all six races of the Southern Ocean Racing Conference, an achievement only she can claim. And since the SORC format has changed recently, this distinction will be hers in perpetuity.

The next decade offered no new challenges for TICONDEROGA. Under several owners, she was chartered for cruises along the eastern seaboard and in the West Indies. It seemed that her racing career had come to an end.

She was rescued from this fate by west coast lumber tycoon Robert Johnson. Realizing her potential, he purchased the aging ketch in 1963. After re-fitting her for serious racing, Johnson assembled an experienced crew and entered TICONDEROGA in the 2,225-mile Transpacific race from Los Angeles to Honolulu that year. She didn't disappoint her new owner and won handily. In 1964, TICONDEROGA broke the record for the 3,600-mile Tahiti race, established two years earlier by the 16-foot longer MORNING STAR.

But TICONDEROGA's greatest moment of glory was yet to come. Among the contestants entered in the 1965 Transpacific was the 73-foot Dutch ketch STORMVOGEL, a renowned racer. The two yachts were evenly matched. After covering over 2,000 miles of Pacific in a strong northeasterly trade wind, they closed in on Hawaii within hailing distance. Running down Molokai channel under spinnaker before a 40-knot gale they engaged in a spectacular duel. Both yachts were clocking speeds of 20 knots as they surfed toward Honolulu in 30-foot seas. TI, as she was affectionately called by now, swept across the finish line at the Diamond Head buoy 5 minutes and 48 seconds ahead of her much younger rival. Winning the Transpacific race for a second time, she also clipped over an hour off the "unbreakable" course record, held by the 88-foot MORNING STAR for 12 years.

Setting new blue water racing records have made TICONDEROGA a legend in her own time. Her sharp cutwater slicing across Narragansett Bay, she diplays the classic "Herreshoff" lines (opposite).

Four out of six races of the Southern Ocean Racing Conference were sailed in the Gulf Stream, which can reach a velocity of over four knots in the Straits of Florida. This presented a challenge to competitors, particularly with strong northerly winds creating steep seas.

The US yacht CELEBRATION is lifted onto a liquid pedestal during the 1983 Miami – Nassau race (above).

The hull of Germany's VINETA disappears momentarily in a trough as she leads the US yacht IMP in the 1979 Ocean Triangle (opposite).

BOOM BOOM, a Class E Morgan 41, sails under reefed main and a high cut Yankee as she claws her way to windward in heavy seas churned up by a strong northerly breeze in the 1981 Ocean Triangle (overleaf).

Since its inception in 1961, the SORC had been dominated by US yachts. The Canadian 40-footer RED JACKET, from the design team of Cuthbertson/Cassian and owned by Perry Connolly of the Royal Canadian Yacht Club in Toronto, was the first non-American yacht to win Overall Honours in 1968. After more than three decades RED JACKET, now owned by Paul J. Phelan of the RCYC, is still a very successful racer on the Great Lakes (opposite, top left).

The German 39-foot yacht DIVA, designed by Joubert/Nivelt and helmed by Berend Beilken of Hamburg was the second "foreigner" to take the trophy of Overall Winner in the SORC of 1984. Here she is seen running down Florida's west coast in the St. Petersburg-Fort Lauderdale race (opposite, top right).

MOTIVATION, 33 feet overall, came from the drawing board of Dutch designer van de Stadt and is owned by Karl v. Wendt. The smallest entry in the SORC of 1984, she won Class E overall and was First in Fleet in the Miami-Nassau race. Here, she is broad reaching under spinnaker in Tampa Bay during the Boca Grande race (opposite, bottom left).

The French Maxi yacht EMERAUDE, a Frers 69 skippered by Jacques Dewailly was Class A winner of the 1986 Miami-Nassau race (opposite, bottom right).

Participants in the 1981 St. Petersburg-Fort Lauderdale long distance race encountered weather conditions so severe that 11 yachts were forced to withdraw with broken masts or other major gear failure. Skipper Anne Gardner and her all-female crew proved their mettle by completing the course in DEUCES WILD, a Heritage 37, seen here as she approaches the finish line at Fort Lauderdale (above).

After the start of the 1981 Miami-Nassau race the fleet had to tack up to Fort Lauderdale Sea Buoy 1, before crossing the Gulf Stream. Bill McAteer's 41-foot Class C yacht IMMIGRANT has just rounded that buoy and is hoisting her spinnaker to catch up to the 47-foot Class B yacht INFINITY, which had started 15 minutes earlier. A late afternoon sun breaks through the clouds to light up this scene (overleaf).

In a display of grace and power two Maxi yachts head south along Florida's west coast in the Boca Grande race of 1981. Jim Kilroy's new 81-footer KIALOA IV was the highest rating yacht entered that year. WINDWARD PASSAGE, a 72-foot seasoned campaigner, is in hot pursuit. KIALOA IV was first across the finish line, but WINDWARD PASSAGE won Class A on handicap (two pages overleaf).

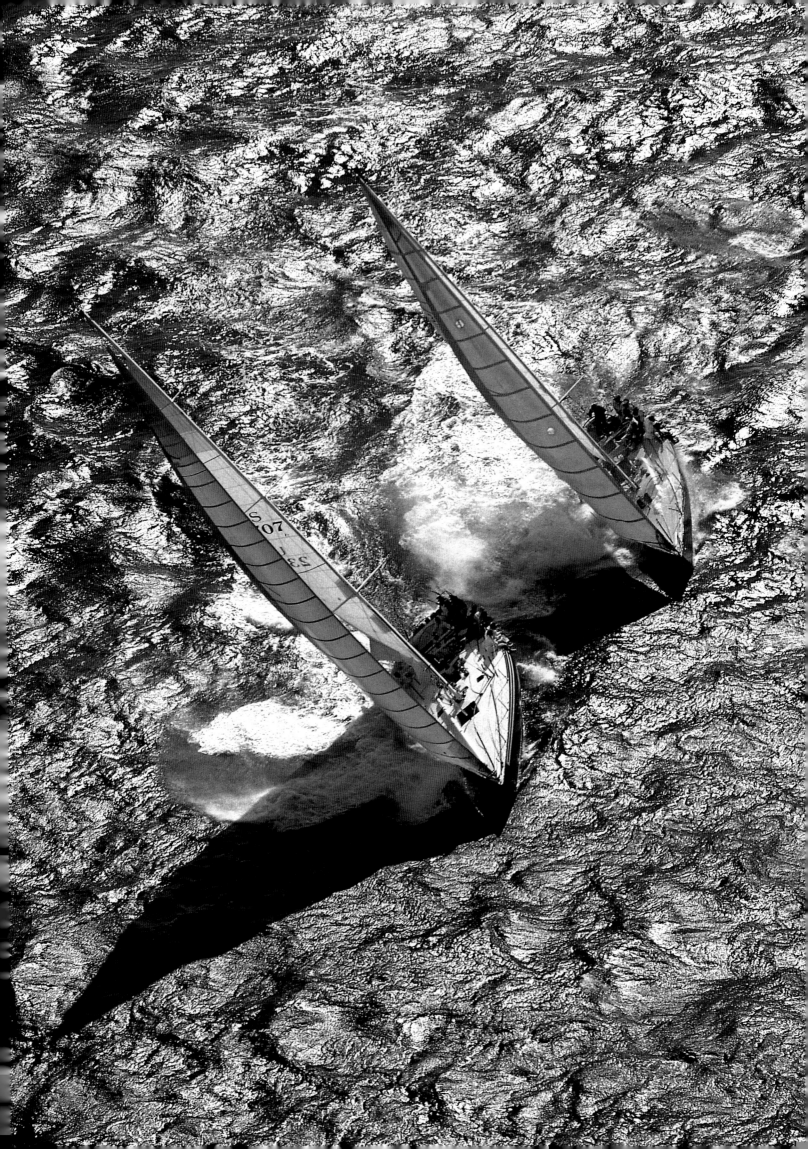

WINDWARD PASSAGE was built on a Bahamian beach. Launched in 1969, the 72-foot veteran of Maxis has been remarkably successful, collecting trophies for several owners. Sailed by the Johnson brothers, she beat the brand new 81-footer KIALOA IV and 11 other Maxis to win the Boca Grande race of 1981. Purchased by Australian Rod Muir in 1985, she continues her racing career in the Southern hemisphere.

With 13 of her 18 crew "railbirding", WINDWARD PASSAGE is racing close-hauled in the 1981 Lipton Cup (preceding pages).

Visual effects created by the interplay of elements and yachts are often remarkable....

Their wakes seem like trailing veils of dancers as four Class C yachts race in a formation that appears to be choreographed (above).

Wind and reflected sunlight combine to produce a striking pattern on the surface of the ocean. Two racing yachts, in harmonious balance, complement nature's design. The Class B yachts MORNING STAR and INTUITION in the 1982 Miami-Nassau race (opposite).

A caprice of the wind can put this balance to the test. Caught by a sudden gust, Ted Turner's Maxi yacht TENACIOUS heels over in a broach and carves a churning wake. Seconds later, she has found her feet again and is on her way to winning the 1979 Ocean Triangle race (overleaf).

Mountains of vulcanic origin look down on Costa Smeralda, the Emerald Coast on the northwestern side of the island of Sardinia. Its craggy shoreline is interspersed with rocky promontories, sandy beaches and sheltered bays. Nestled in the Bay of Porto Cervo is the Villaggio Marina. Once a humble fishing village, it is now one of Europe's most luxurious resorts. The excellent docking and service facilities of its marina have made Porto Cervo a popular destination for sailors from all over the world. The Yacht Club Smeralda has mounted several America's Cup challenges and is headquarters of the Sardinia Cup and many other yachting events of international calibre.

Light winds and sunny skies predominated during the course races of the 1982 Sardinia Cup. In these conditions, progress after the start was slow and it took time for yachts to separate and sail for clear air (above).

After hours on the course the fleet was dispersed over a wide area. A late afternoon sun cast silver ripples across the sea as an onshore breeze carried the leaders toward the finish at Porto Cervo (below).

In the long distance race to Hyères in France, the yacht RECLUTA of Team Argentina made good speed in the Strait of Bonifacio, which separates the Mediterranean islands of Sardinia and Corsica (opposite).

Steady trade winds in the 20 to 25-knot range and an intensely blue Pacific adorned with sparkling whitecaps make course racing for the Clipper Cup off Honolulu a sailor's dream. The 82-foot Maxi SORCERY, designed by Gary Mull and owned by Jacob Wood of the Waikiki Yacht Club on the island of Oahu, was the largest and highest rating entry in the Kenwood Clipper Cup of 1986. Placing first in four out of five races, she was also the Overall winner of Class A.

With her spinnaker trimmed perfectly to a 20-knot breeze, the red yacht leads the fleet on her way to the downwind mark of the third triangle race (opposite).

EXADOR, a 40-footer designed by New Zealand's Bruce Farr, was the Overall winner in Class D. With her team mates, EQUITY and THUNDERBIRD – which were also drawn by Bruce Farr – she claimed the highest prize of the series, the Team Trophy of the 1986 Kenwood Clipper Cup for New Zealand. EQUITY was the Overall winner in Class C.

EXADOR is owned by Michael Clark of the Royal Akarana Yacht Club. Here she is off to an early lead at the start of the first triangle race, setting the pace for Team New Zealand. EXADOR stayed ahead to get the gun in her division (above).

A first place finish in the middle distance Molokai race and high placings in the four other races secured an Overall win in Class B for Basil Twist's yacht BLADE RUNNER from the Saint Francis Yacht Club in San Francisco. In the fleet overall standings she placed a very respectable fourth.

The Koolau mountain range of Oahu rises in the background as BLADE RUNNER, B. Twist's 47-footer designed by the team of Reichel/Pugh reaches with her rainbow colour spinnaker in the second triangle race. She is hard on the heels of another Class B yacht, TOMAHAWK, a design of German Frers. The 51-footer is owned by John Arens and sails out of the Balboa Yacht Club in Panama (overleaf).

CRAZY HORSE, a Nelson/Marek designed 49-footer owned by Larry Harvey of the San Diego Yacht Club, closing in on Kauwai in the Around the State race.

CRAZY HORSE took home trophies for winning Class B and Best Individual Yacht of the 1986 Clipper Cup series (opposite).

While photographing windsurfers at Diamond Head, I noticed Clipper Cup yachts heading toward the shore after the start of the Molokai race. Swimming out about a mile, I got a close-up of the Japanese Class C entry RURIKO (above).

The 775 mile Around the State race can claim to be the longest of the Grand Prix Circuit. The topography of the Hawaiian archipelago always presents a challenge to the fleet. Wind conditions vary from fair trades in the open ocean to light and fickle air on the leeward side of mountainous islands. In the Molokai channel, a breeze can reach gale force.

In 1986 the Japanese Class B yacht ZERO, a Frers 52 owned by S. Tsumura, was first Overall. To avoid a broach, she lets her full mainsail run out (right).

The final contest of the Southern Cross Cup is the popular Sydney-Hobart race, which has been held annually since 1945. It is open to all yachts that meet the safety standard of the Cruising Yacht Club of Australia. The course leads from Sydney harbour to Hobart on the Derwent river in Tasmania, a distance of 630 nautical miles. This race can be a severe test for yacht and crew. Gale force winds are common in Bass Strait, between the southern tip of Australia and the north shore of the island of Tasmania, as well as in Storm Bay at the approach to Hobart.

The gun for the 1981 Sydney-Hobart race went off at 1 PM on Boxing Day, sending 163 yachts, ranging in size from 32 to 81 feet, on their way to the capital of the island of Tasmania. At the half-mile long starting line off Shark Point in Sydney harbour the wind was over the starboard beam, calling for some tricky spinnaker flying at close quarters as the fleet reached toward the harbour entrance, guarded by Sydney's North and South Heads (opposite, top).

Approaching a turning mark vessel anchored off Hornby Light, yachts had to take down their spinnakers rapidly, as they now had to go hard on the wind to gain the open Pacific. Yachts bearing down on the mark under spinnaker completely obscure the large mark vessel, while yachts in the background have already rounded the mark and are close hauled. In the distance the suburb of Manly on Sydney's North Head peninsula (opposite, bottom).

Eleven national teams from Australia, England, Hong Kong, New Zealand, Papua New Guinea and one from each of the six Australian States vied for the 1981 Southern Cross Cup, a combination of two course races, a middle distance race of 180 miles and the Sydney-Hobart race.

The 40-footer HITCHHIKER, a yacht from the drawing board of Brazilian designer German Frers, is owned by P. Briggs of the Royal Perth Yacht Club of Western Australia. HITCHHIKER not only scored first place in her class for the middle distance and Sydney-Hobart race, but she and her team-mates, RAGAMUFFIN and APOLLO V, secured the Southern Cross Cup for Team Australia.

HITCHHIKER, hard on the wind in the second course race of the Southern Cross Cup (above).

Australia's expectations for Bernard Lewis' Maxi yacht VENGEANCE to break the US Maxi KIALOA's 1975 record of two days, 14 hours and 37 seconds for the 630-mile Sydney-Hobart course were not fulfilled. Storm Bay would not live up to its name as VENGEANCE ran toward Hobart in light air. Although taking line honours and winning Class A, she placed a disappointing 33rd on corrected time (opposite).

The same fate befell Bob Bell's Maxi CONDOR OF BERMUDA, as she reached up the mouth of the Derwent River, marked by a bizarre rock formation known as the "Organ Pipes" (overleaf).

SOLANDRA, of the Royal Yacht Club of Tasmania and owned by Reg Escott, crossed the finish line at her home port at 2.48 AM on New Year's Day, 5 seconds behind ZEUSS II, to place a remarkable second overall in the 1981 Sydney-Hobart race. This sturdy 32-footer, built of Tasmanian Huon pine, faced winds up to 40 knots in Bass Strait without experiencing any gear failure. Unlike their larger sisters she, and most of the smaller yachts, profited from a breeze of 25 knots as they entered Storm Bay, which reflected favourably on their corrected time.

On January 2, 1982, a mere 30 hours after completing a demanding 630-mile Sydney-Hobart race, SOLANDRA raced in the "King of the Derwent" regatta (above).

After the start from the Royal Yacht Squadron at Cowes in the first race of the 1979 Admiral's Cup, some yachts took a chance by sailing precipitously close inshore. This had the advantage of making use of a counter current at the edge of a strong incoming tide that ran up the Solent. But it was a gamble. Hard groundings and damaged keels were frequently the result. To secure overnight service, the repair facilities of Groves & Gutteridge at West Cowes had to be booked by VHF radio while the damaged yacht was still sailing.

Tacking down the Solent at close quarters and within feet of the shore (opposite, top).

The German yacht RUBIN bears off as she is rounding Hamstead Ledge buoy. Canada's MAGISTRI and IMPETUOUS of Australia, both on starboard tack, approach the buoy. MAGISTRI, with "inside overlap rights", luffs up IMPETUOUS to lay the mark. INCISIF of Belgium is on port tack and has no chance to squeeze by. She must lay off and take the stern of MAGISTRI and IMPETUOUS before tacking over to fetch the mark (opposite, bottom).

The Solent is veritable steeplechase of strong tides, counter currents, rocky shoals, mudbanks and traffic, ranging from giant tankers to small pleasure craft.

The Royal yacht BRITANNIA, anchored in the race course, is just one more hurdle competitors in the Admiral's Cup must overcome. ASSIDUOUS of Switzerland and GEKKO of Japan have to tack across her stately bow (above).

A stiff breeze brings out the "white horses" as the fleet runs downwind under spinnaker in the second race. Brazil's entry INDIGO, a 46-footer designed by German Frers, is in the foreground (overleaf).

In the second course race of the Admiral's Cup, England's largest yacht, BLIZZARD, leads the fleet of 57 Admiral's Cup yachts. Unfortunately she is heading for the wrong mark (preceding pages).

Later in the same race, Australia's POLICE CAR smartly overhauls BLIZZARD on the English yacht's windward side. Rather than reef it, POLICE CAR carries her fully hoisted mainsail. In a gust like this one, the main is ragged to de-power it to prevent excessive heeling (opposite, top).

JAN POTT of Germany is caught in a precarious roll on the downwind leg of the first course race as her foredeck crew is about to gybe the spinnaker (opposite, bottom).

Admiral's Cup yachts parade their spinnakers at the start of the 1979 Channel Race, a 217-mile middle distance contest leading from Cowes to the Cherbourg buoy on the French coast and back to the Solent (above).

RAGAMUFFIN sweeps downwind under flying sails and reefed main. She and team mates POLICE CAR and IMPETUOUS took the Admiral's Cup to Australia in 1979 (right).

Sometimes, the camera catches a fleeting moment of symmetry in the constantly changing scenery of yacht racing.
IMPETUOUS of Australia can claim "buoy room" over the yacht ASSIDUOUS of Switzerland and Belgium's INCISIF and tack around Clipper buoy (preceding pages).

In the third course race, Admiral's Cup contestants had to share the Solent with much smaller yachts competing in the popular Cowes Week regatta (opposite, top).

The Spanish entries, TORNADO and YACHTMAN, bowling downwind in the third race (opposite, bottom left).

England's ECLIPSE, a Contessa 39 built and skippered by Jeremy Rogers, was the highest scoring yacht in the 1979 Admiral's Cup. One of the smallest yachts entered, she took first place among Cup contenders in the storm-ridden Fastnet race. ECLIPSE was named Yacht of the Year for her remarkable achievement (opposite, bottom right).

Light air at the start of the 1979 Fastnet race gave no indication of an impending disaster. Caught in the open sea between Land's End and the southern tip of Ireland, the largest fleet ever assembled in yacht racing history was ravaged by an unpredictable Force 11 storm. 60-knot winds and 40-foot waves claimed five yachts and fifteen lives. Only 85 of 303 yachts were able to complete the 605-mile race. Nineteen yachts had to be abandoned and 194, among them the German Admiral's Cup yacht TINA, in the foreground, retired (above).

Seas were still running high after the storm, when the Maxi yachts ran down the coast of Cornwall toward the finish of the Fastnet race at Plymouth. CONDOR OF BERMUDA took line honours (overleaf, left).

But Ted Turner's TENACIOUS was the Overall winner on corrected time. Turner missed breaking the course record of 79 hours and 12 minutes he had set in 1971 with the converted 12-Meter AMERICAN EAGLE by 41 minutes (overleaf, right).

LEVEL RACING

Whereas competing under a handicap system remains the most popular form of yacht racing from small club regattas to the international Grand Prix circuit, it has one inherent disadvantage. Because yachts of different sizes compete against each other, the first boat to cross the finish line might not be the victor. Although a computer program can establish the final results within minutes, the eventual winner cannot be determined until the last yacht has completed the race, sometimes hours after the fastest competitors have already finished. The last yacht home might indeed be first, if she had been sailed to her potential.

This was not considered satisfactory by sailors who wanted close racing and immediate results. It led to the introduction of "Level Racing". Although boats were not identical as in class racing, they had to conform to parameters that allowed little, if any, performance advantage. The first One-Ton World Cup was held in 1965, followed by the Half-Ton Cup in 1966 and the Two-Ton and Quarter-Ton Cup in 1967. The designation "Ton" is misleading inasmuch as it does not refer to the displacement, but to the approximate size of a yacht. Two-Tonners are about 40 feet long and Quarter-Tonners are around 25 feet.

The most ambitious endeavour in level racing was the 50-Foot class, a concept of Swedish industrialist Wictor Forss. Introduced in 1989, twelve yachts from four countries competed. Requiring a crew of thirteen, some of these sleek racers were constructed of ultra-light, but strong carbon fibre and titanium. A series of seven contests was held in Japan, the Caribbean and the United States to determine the International 50-Foot World Champion. By 1990, seven countries participated and the class had grown to 29. But it was divided into Gold and Silver fleets, because some of the only one-year-old yachts had already lost their competitive edge. A victim of exorbitant cost, World Championship competition ceased in 1991.

Start of the inaugural race of the 50-Foot class at Key West in January of 1989. CARAT, on the right of the picture, is owned by Wictor Forss. She won this race, the series and the World Championship that year (opposite, top).

PROFESSIONAL RACING

The "Ultimate 30" was a notion of the US Professional Sailing Association. Its parameters were few: a monohull not exceeding a length of 30 feet, a maximum beam of 14 feet and a minimum weight of 2,000 pounds. The crew of six to eight hiked out on a platform to keep the boat, which had no limitation in sail area and flew an enormous spinnaker, from capsizing. Given the right wind conditions, Ultimate 30s routinely travelled at over 20 knots. This speed would make for exciting inshore racing and draw spectators, the USPSA argued. Between 1988 and 1990 four to five annual events were held in Corpus Christie, San Francisco, Milwaukee, Annapolis and Hawaii, under the overall sponsorship of storage bag manufacturer Ziploc. Beyond that, the crew of each participating boat had to find their own sponsors. In 1989, the top scoring Ultimate 30 earned $116,665 in prize money.

Unfortunately, at times the breeze would refuse to co-operate on the days of a scheduled event. The 1990 contest at the resort of Turtle Bay on the north shore of Oahu was sailed in very light air, while during a practice race just the day before the wind had been blowing so strongly that the skipper of one of the 30s reported having had difficulty avoiding a collision with a breaching whale.

Lack of media coverage and spectator participation led to the end of these contests.

To escape a thunderstorm, three Ultimate 30s reach toward shelter at Haleiwa harbour on the north shore of Oahu, Hawaii (opposite, bottom).

ANTIGUA SAILING WEEK

Complementing the serious racing scene, there are regattas which cater to a broader spectrum of yachts by using a more flexible handicapping system. A prime example is the tremendously popular annual Antigua Sailing Week, which celebrated its 30th anniversary in 1997 with a record 256 entries from 31 countries. The recipe for this resounding success is simple: sailors unable to bring their own yacht to Antigua can participate by making arrangements with one of the excellent charter services on the island. To accommodate such a great variety of sailing vessels, the international fleet is divided into three classes: racing, cruising and traditional yachts. The racing class – from 72-foot Maxis to 24-foot Minis – sails a somewhat longer course than the other two classes, but the finish line for all classes is at the same location. The prevailing 15 to 20-knot trade winds practically guarantee that all participating yachts reach the destination of each of the five contests by mid-afternoon. The organizers' reason for strictly adhering to this schedule became evident to me after the very first race. On Antigua, "apres race" shoreside activities with barbecues, steel bands and rum punch parties continue well past midnight and can be more demanding than the sailing.

At English Harbour, Nelson's Dockyard, the Admiral's Inn and splendid colonial mansions are reminders of the 18th century, when a young Nelson made this safe port the headquarters of the British Navy in the Leeward Islands. Now English Harbour is one of the favourite destinations for yachts visiting the Caribbean and the headquarters of more peaceful activities – the Antigua Sailing Week. Starting from here, the first race follows the undulating western shore of the island to finish at Dickenson Bay. A 17-mile triangle off Halcyon Cove is sailed the next day. Race three is the reverse of the first course, ending at English Harbour and race four crisscrosses the south coast to finish at Curtain Bluff Cove. The final race is once more almost a reversal of the fourth race, leading back to English Harbour.

There was no motor boat left for rent on the island, but I had no difficulty finding a cruising class yacht that took me on as crew. Jim Hearl, owner of MOON SHADOW, a well appointed Gulfstar 50, welcomed me aboard. A manufacturer of electronic components from Salem, Massachusetts, Jim turned out to be a most generous host. He was also a staunch proponent of the principle that participation is more important than winning. His crew, consisting of friends with limited, if any, sailing experience, did not contribute much to our effort. Despite a generous rating we never placed well. As it turned out, this worked to my advantage, because it gave me ample opportunity to take shots of our competitors as they passed us at will. My assignment was to winch in the sheet of the Gulfstar's substantial genoa, a formidable task that whipped me into top shape. Jim's yacht was kept Bristol fashion by a professional sailor, whose wife was an excellent cook and served up the most delicious meals en route.

Reluctantly I abandoned MOON SHADOW's carefree atmosphere after four days to take some aerial shots of the last race. The cover photograph was the reward for my selfless decision.

Antigua Sailing Week winds up with Dockyard Day, an afternoon of fun and relaxation. It includes events such as the Non-Mariners Race in vessels constructed of the most unlikely materials imaginable, Walking the Greasy Pole, a Tug-O-War and, to quote from the official programme, "general hell raising". The awards banquet and Lord Nelson's Ball conclude Antigua Sailing Week – a true test of stamina.

The racing class rounds a headland of Antigua's west coast (opposite, top).
PANACEA, a Morgan 52, passes MOON SHADOW on the leeward side (opposite, bottom).

Antigua Sailing Week premiered in 1967, when 24 yachts participated in the event. From these inconspicuous beginnings the number of entries has increased steadily year by year. In 1997, the island experienced an invasion of 256 yachts. Serious racers sail a longer course than less ambitious cruisers; when the yachts are anchored for the night, all stay the long course at lively shoreside parties.

The Venezuelan yacht ABRACADABRA, a Swan 43 built in Finland, spreads her flying sails like wings of a tropical bird as she rushes downwind past Hawksbill (opposite).

Close hauled under a reefed main MISTRAL, an Aage Nielson 50 hailing from Gloucester, shows us her stern as she leaves MOON SHADOW in her wake (above).

"Photo-finish". The yacht CRACKERJACK of Canadian Walter Zweig edges out TIGER'S KISS from Tortola by a nose across the finish line at Curtain Bluff (overleaf, left).

ANTIDOTE, a J/24 from the US Virgin Islands, skippered by J. Foster, was the smallest and lowest rating yacht in the racing class. But on handicap she managed to take first place from the 72-foot Maxi MISTRESS QUICKLY of Bermuda, the highest rating yacht in the racing fleet. It was a close contest – only two points separated David from Goliath.

ANTIDOTE on her way to victory in the last race of the 1980 Antigua Sailing Week (overleaf, right).

THE CHAMPIONSHIP OF SAILORS

The Championship of Sailors was raced in Nassau Harbour as an anti-climactic appendix to the SORC. World class skippers like Ted Turner, Dennis Conner, Lowell North, Ted Hood, Tom Blackaller and Buddy Melges were invited to demonstrate their sailing skills by competing against the local champions in Bahama Sloops.

The Caribbean version of high-tech racers, these colourful craft are equipped with an enormous mainsail and a narrow jib. The most striking feature is a movable hiking plank that can be extended far beyond the beam. This board is solid enough to permit up to 10 members of the crew to counterbalance the Bahama Sloop when she is going upwind or close reaching.

It was not uncommon that one of the crew on the hiking plank lost his hold and took a tumble. Fortunately, only his ego suffered; the turquoise waters of Nassau Harbour are temperate and he was promptly "rescued" by one of the numerous spectator boats.

In addition, each sloop carried a fair number of sackcloth bags filled with sand which, depending on prevailing wind conditions, could be used as movable ballast or simply tossed overboard.

Communication between invited skippers, who were allowed to bring only their own tactician aboard, and the all-Bahamian crew was somewhat less than perfect. This would inevitably lead to flagrant rule infractions, heated shouting matches and frequent hull contact.

These "races", extensively covered by the local media, were hilarious affairs and drew more spectators than the Nassau Cup.

At the sound of the gun, anchors are hauled up and sails are hoisted in a "Le Mans" start, an unusual practice in yacht racing (opposite, top).

Bahama Sloop racing at close quarters. Ted Turner, wearing his trademark engineer's cap, is about to tack his dark-hulled sloop (opposite, bottom).

With eight of his crew hiking out on the plank and his tactician keeping a sharp lookout, Tom Blackaller, hidden behind the huge mainsail, steers his Bahama Sloop toward the finish line in first place. Besting not only his SORC competitors, but also the foremost Bahamian skippers, earned him the title "Champion of Sailors" in 1979 (overleaf).

THE AMERICA'S CUP

"It is a remarkable incident and not satisfactory to the national pride" commented the London Spectator. The "incident" took place on August 22, 1851, when the rakish Yankee schooner AMERICA soundly trounced the Royal Yacht Squadron's fastest yachts in a race around the Isle of Wight.

Ironically, it was an Englishman who had suggested to the Americans they should enter a yacht in this race for a new 100 guinea cup, held in connection with the first World's Fair in London. John Cox Stevens, commodore of the only eight year old New York Yacht Club, was intrigued. He formed a syndicate which commissioned noted designer George Steers to build a yacht on the lines of the swift New York pilot schooners. The AMERICA, completed in June of 1851, immediately set sail for Europe and crossed the Atlantic in 20 days.

The cup – 134 ounces of Sterling silver wrought in ornate Victorian scrolls – was taken to the United States aboard the triumphant schooner and handed into the stewardship of the New York Yacht Club. Named the "America's Cup", it would become the symbol of yachting supremacy and the oldest contested trophy in the history of sport.

To restore Britain's tarnished image as a leader in the sport of gentlemen, the Royal Thames Yacht Club sent CAMBRIA across the pond in 1870, confident she would "fetch the Cup back to where it belonged". Alas, the challenger finished a disappointing tenth in a schooner race held off New York.

Match racing, a duel between two yachts only, was introduced in 1871. Precluding interference by other contestants on the race course, it is considered the fairest form of competition under sail. The British schooner LIVONIA never posed a danger to the American defender COLUMBIA that year. Two Canadian challenges in 1876 and 1881 were equally unsuccessful. With a tenacity symbolized by her national mascot, the bulldog, Britain continued her quest for the elusive ewer. However, between 1885 and 1937, American ingenuity prevailed 12 times over English determination. Public interest on both sides of the ocean increased with each match series. Colourful characters, fine sportsmanship and, at times, intrigue provided a wealth of stories for the press. Wrote one reporter after a hotly disputed and eventually disallowed protest: "Britannia rules the waves, but the New York Yacht Club waives the rules". Tea king Sir Thomas Lipton launched five well organized attempts to wrest the "Auld Mug" from its seemingly permanent mooring. Sir Thomas' nemesis proved to be the American yacht designer Nathanael Green Herreshoff, the Wizard of Bristol, Rhode Island. Herreshoff combined sound engineering with an artist's intuition. All of the numerous fast and graceful yachts he drew bore the unmistakable hallmark of his genius, known as "Herreshoff" lines. Nathanael obliged the Americans with superior designs for their defenders, among them RELIANCE, the biggest sloop ever launched. Measuring an astounding 204 feet from bowsprit to boom end, she carried 16,159 square feet of canvas. It took several hands of a crew of 64 just to haul in the 1,000-foot long sheet of her enormous mainsail.

In 1930 it was decided to move the contest away from New York's busy shipping lanes to Rhode Island. The burghers of Newport, a 16th century town nestled among rocky hills and green slopes at the mouth of Narragansett Bay, were no strangers to rubbing shoulders with affluence. Perched above the famous Cliff Walk and strung along shady Belleview Avenue were the magnificent marble and cut stone summer retreats of the eastern seaboard's industrial tycoons and financial nobility. Most of these lavish mansions date back to the late 19th century and were referred to as "cottages" by their owners – a hint at form and a proclivity for understatement.

"J" Class yachts, sleek giants with masts reaching up to a lofty 185 feet from the waterline, were the weapons of the day. The first real threat to the Cup defenders came in 1934. The ENDEAVOUR of British aviation magnate T.O.M. Sopwith was a very fast boat and took a two to zero lead over the Americans' RAINBOW. A third win would have given ENDEAVOUR the Cup. She held a narrow lead until halfway into the final leg of that race. But a shrewd tactical manoeuvre saved the day for the defenders. RAINBOW crossed the finish line less than a minute ahead and went on to win the next three races.

Recognizing that the cost of "J" Class boats had become prohibitive in a decade of economic uncertainty following World War II, the New York Yacht Club concluded that a smaller yacht had to be selected, if Cup competition was to continue. Their choice, the 12-Meter Class, proved to be an excellent one. The term "12-Meter" is misleading; the average overall length of a 12-Meter is about 21 meters or 69 feet. The 12-Meter rule equation, to which a yacht must conform, permits a certain flexibility in design without endangering fair racing, as it produces boats very similar in appearance and speed.

Although the scene was now set for some close competition, four challenges between 1958 and 1967 – two each from England and Australia – turned out to be one-sided affairs. Even with their potentially superior GRETL, the Australians were tactically outfoxed by the defenders in 1962. With the outcome of each new challenge so predictable, public interest began to wane. "Seeing two boats doing the same thing all over again is about as exciting as watching paint dry", observed one disgruntled spectator. The pulse quickened somewhat in 1970 with the appearance of Baron Marcel Bich, monarch of a worldwide ballpoint pen empire, who joined the Australians in a bid for that year's challenge. He returned three times. His Twelves, all named FRANCE, never made it beyond the elimination rounds. However, the Baron's lavish parties in one of the mansions on Belleview Avenue and on his luxuriously appointed yacht SHENANDOAH were the social events of a Cup season.

1977 was the year of sweet revenge for Ted Turner, the effervescent self-made millionaire from Atlanta. Voted "Yachtsman of the Year" three times, the dynamic Southerner had won more than his share of races in boats ranging from dinghies to his Maxi yacht TENACIOUS. In 1974 he had been "excused" by the New York Yacht Club's selection committee from further competition in the defenders' elimination series when his Twelve, MARINER, showed a pronounced lack of speed. That experience had left a bitter taste in Turner's mouth. This time he was at the helm of COURAGEOUS, the successful defender of the 1974 campaign. And this time, sailing with a vengeance, he won the right to defend. A dashing figure on and off the water, handsome Ted's choice remarks and uninhibited style provided a refreshing contrast to the august atmosphere of restrained exclusivity which the New York yachting establishment had preserved so punctiliously for more than a century. Turner's flamboyance was the spark needed to rekindle public interest. The media, thankful for the opportunity, reported every word he spoke and every move he made. "Cup Fever" spread from Newport across the United States; "Captain Courageous" T-shirts and "Turner for President" buttons sold by the thousands. Folk hero Turner obliged by dispatching the Australians, who had eliminated France and Sweden, with a perfect score of four straight wins.

Dennis Conner, defending with FREEDOM in 1980, was cut from a different cloth. No extrovert, he approached the task at hand with the precision of a neurosurgeon. The Australians, who once more had prevailed by eliminating England, France and Sweden, managed to take only one race from FREEDOM and lost the contest four to one. Remarked one weary reporter: "Conner has lifted this event to the pinnacle of boredom". It had been the 24th consecutive defence by the New York Yacht Club. It also had been a personal triumph for Olim Stephens, the American designer of all winning Twelves since 1958.

The contest of 1983 was of another flavour again, but for different reasons. The cost of a Cup campaign had become exorbitant. "If you have to ask the price of a yacht you can't afford it". J.P. Morgan's quip of yesteryear rang more true than ever. Individual financing was augmented or totally replaced by corporate sponsorship, although, in keeping with the Corinthian image yachting had always projected, advertising was unobtrusive. Only the French Baron and Alan Bond, an English immigrant, who had struck it rich in Western Australia, footed the bill personally. Electronics also made their debut; all contestants sported sophisticated on-board computers which registered even the slightest changes in a yacht's performance. And crews lived like cadets in dorms, every minute of their day filled with fitness training, sailing practice and morale boosting sessions. This time even the Australians were put under curfew; the ever so popular beer bashes of the challengers from "down under" and their entourage at Christie's belonged to the past. Participation was at an all time high. Four American boats vied for the honour to defend. Three Australian challengers and one each from Canada, England, France and Italy crossed tacks for the right to challenge.

The story of the year, however, was the secrecy surrounding the keel of Alan Bond's 12-Meter AUSTRALIA II. Customarily, all yachts would be hoisted from the water after each day's battle to be scrubbed – in full view of anyone who cared to admire these marvels of marine architecture. Not so

AUSTRALIA II; a curtain shrouded her "winged" keel like a veil hiding the charms of a bashful maiden. The yacht's performance caused considerable concern in the defender's camp. Although she officially measured in under the rule, the Americans protested her unseen keel. The protest made headlines, was finally disallowed and did little to enhance the spirit of fair competition. The sentiment of the Newport crowd, including quite a few Americans, who in previous years had always doted on their defenders, registered a marked swing toward the maligned challenger.

Skippered by John Bertrand, AUSTRALIA II prevailed in the challengers' eliminations by ousting her opponents from Canada, England, France, Italy and Australia. Dennis Conner's new LIBERTY eliminated her two rivals on the defenders' side. The final confrontation was a cliff-hanger. AUSTRALIA had a slight speed advantage, but lost the first two races due to gear failure. At the end of six very close matches the contest was tied three to three. In the deciding seventh race, the lead changed twice on the first beat and LIBERTY rounded the weather mark 29 seconds ahead of her opponent. She managed to increase her lead on both reaches and the second weather leg, rounding the top mark with a 57-second advantage. But on the crucial downwind leg AUSTRALIA II went to the right of the rhumb line, searching for better wind. And this tactical move paid off. At the last mark, AUSTRALIA II was ahead of LIBERTY by 21 seconds. The final beat to the finish line was a continuous battle. Trying to break Bertrand's cover, Conner forced a total of 47 tacks. To no avail – the Australians got the gun and took the Cup. A spell that had lasted for 132 years was finally broken.

A tidal wave of euphoria swept across Australia, a country where sailing is a major pastime, minutes after her yacht crossed the finish line. Bertrand, his crew and the obstinate trophy received a tumultuous welcome. With the America's Cup held by the Royal Perth Yacht Club now, the venue of the next contest would be the Indian Ocean off Freemantle.

Certain parallels between Newport and Freemantle are obvious: the solid stone structures of public buildings are similar in style and bear witness to the fact that both towns were settled by British colonists. The fishing boats which provide local restaurants with the catch of the day and the down-to-earth people, hospitable, always ready to lend a helping hand to the visitor. There are differences too. When Newport goes to lunch, Freemantle, half way around the globe, goes to bed. And when the grey combers of winter crash into New England's eastern seaboard, Western Australia's beaches bask in a bright summer sun.

However, the difference of considerable concern to the challengers was that of the wind charts. In Newport's Narragansett Bay, a light to medium summer breeze is to be expected, whereas the "Freemantle Doctor", a lusty 20 to 30-knot southwesterly pays his visit to Gage Road about noon each day with astounding punctuality. This wind churns up wickedly steep seas, powerful enough to sweep a crew off the deck of a 12-Meter and into the green-blue Indian Ocean. There would be a change of pace.

In October of 1986, Freemantle sparkled with fresh paint. An unprecedented number of yachts, 13 in all, from the United States, France, Italy, England, Canada and New Zealand started a series of gruelling round robin matches for the right to challenge. Meanwhile, five Australian Twelves battled each other to determine the defender. These eliminations continued until January of 1987. Well-organized race committees executed the daily task of coordinating eight match races on three courses, allocating support vessels and keeping the large spectator fleet in check with clockwork precision. Reporters who preferred terra firma to the bone-rattling jolts of a press boat could follow the action live in the dry comfort of the IBM media centre. Half a dozen large television screens showed spinnakers exploding in 40-knot gusts and foredeck hands, buried to their shoulders in solid green water, hanging on for dear life.

On the challengers' side, four yachts emerged to qualify for the semi-final round. NEW ZEALAND led this series with an impressive record of 34 wins against only five losses and had to be considered the favourite. As expected, she dispatched FRENCH KISS to advance to the finals. STARS & STRIPES, helmed by Dennis Conner, had worked her way into second place after a rather inconspicuous performance in the initial rounds. Conner, this time sailing for the San Diego Yacht Club and determined to return the Cup to the United States, was backed by a syndicate which had financed the most extensive design and training program in 12-Meter history. He beat AMERICA II of the New York Yacht Club to face NEW ZEALAND in the challengers' finals. This was expected to be a close contest, but STARS & STRIPES won in four straight to become the challenger. In the Australian camp, KOOKABURRA III had established an edge over her four rivals and was selected the defending yacht.

Onboard television cameras transmitted the dramatic scene of flying spray, straining muscles and tense faces. Yachting fans from all over the world were able to witness live broadcasts of Dennis Conner's astounding comeback. STARS & STRIPES defeated KOOKABURRA III in a clean sweep and recaptured the America's Cup for the United States. The locale for the next defence would be Conner's home waters off San Diego.

Freemantle was to be the end of the 12-Meter Class. The next challenge was mounted by Michael Fay, an investment banker from New Zealand. Fay had found a loophole in the "Deed of Gift" of the New York Yacht Club, which contains the definition of a yacht eligible for Cup competition. One would like to think that this elaborate document should leave no doubt as to the criteria of such a vessel. Obviously this was not the case. Fay turned up in San Diego with a craft resembling a floating football field rather than a sailing vessel. He insisted that New Zealand would win the Cup by default, if his challenge was not accepted. The issue was hotly contested by the Americans. After prolonged legal battles in lower courts, the New York Supreme Court found for the challenger. Compelled to defend or forfeit the Cup, the San Diego Yacht Club stole a page from Fay's book and, referring to the same document, countered with a catamaran. The outcome was as expected: Dennis Conner made short shrift of the New Zealand monster by crossing the finish line with an inordinate lead in every race. I chose not to cover this farce.

To forestall the recurrence of such an obvious mismatch, yachts of a newly created International America's Cup Class were agreed upon for the 1992 and 1995 Cup competitions. Larger than the Twelves, they also carried a much higher price tag. By now the cost of a Cup campaign could run up to $60 million. What once had been the sport of gentlemen turned into a fierce contest for financial backing. However, commercial sponsors, who in the past had been content with limited exposure, now insisted that their trademarks be displayed prominently on the yacht they supported. This was not permitted under a rule of the International Yacht Racing Union. To assure the continuance of America's Cup competition the rule was changed. Sails, hulls, even booms were emblazoned with logos of the corporate world, ranging from airlines and automobile manufacturers to producers of cranberry juice and yogurt.

Concerning the action on the water a comparison with Freemantle was inevitable. The new America's Cup Class yachts were inherently faster than the old Twelves. But the wind of southern California could not provide the excitement of heavy weather racing. In the light to medium air that prevailed off Point Loma in San Diego the new yachts, with their huge mainsails and spinnakers the size of two tennis courts, resembled floating billboards. Therefore, the 1987 event in Australia, which also featured the largest number of competing America's Cup yachts, is given pictorial preference in this book.

In 1992, the Americans retained the Cup with Bill Koch's AMERICA^3 , a superior yacht that out-classed Dennis Conner's new STARS & STRIPES in the defender's trials and handily beat the eventual challenger IL MORO DI VENEZIA of Italy in the finals.

In 1995, New Zealander Peter Blake mounted a superb campaign. TEAM NEW ZEALAND, helmed by Russell Coutts, eliminated challengers from six countries with a score of 46 wins and only one loss. Awed by the Kiwis' impressive performance, two of the American defender syndicates decided to join forces – a hitherto unthinkable move – in an attempt to keep the America's Cup in San Diego. Although Conner and his crew had qualified in the latest version of STARS & STRIPES, they were given the faster yacht YOUNG AMERICA of the New York Yacht Club. It was to no avail. Leading at every mark in each race, TEAM NEW ZEALAND humbled YOUNG AMERICA with a five to nil drubbing. After only twelve years, yachting's ultimate trophy found its way to the southern hemisphere for a second time.

The next America's Cup challenge will be sailed in New Zealand, in latitudes known for heavy seas and strong winds – conditions that virtually guarantee a fascinating contest.

The AMERICA's victory over the fastest yachts of the Royal Yacht Squadron in a race around the Isle of Wight in 1851 precipitated a perpetual tourney for supremacy in yacht racing. Known as the "America's Cup", it is now the oldest contested trophy in the history of sport. An exact replica of the AMERICA was launched in 1967. Demonstrating AMERICA's swiftness, the replica sails upwind in light air at the remarkable speed of six knots (opposite).

In 1974, the 12-Meter COURAGEOUS, skippered by Ted Hood, successfully defended the Cup for the United States against the Australian challenger SOUTHERN CROSS with a score of four to zero in the best of seven contest (above).

Ted Turner purchased COURAGEOUS for the 1977 Cup defence. Dispatching AUSTRALIA in four straight wins, COURAGEOUS kept the Cup in America for a second time.
Ahead of her rival, COURAGEOUS is reaching for the gybe mark (overleaf).

Sir James Hardy, at the helm of AUSTRALIA, managed to score one win against Dennis Conner's FREEDOM in 1980. This was quite an accomplishment, considering that AUSTRALIA was the

modified campaigner of 1977, which had been beaten decisively by an already five year old COURAGEOUS that year, whereas FREEDOM was a state-of-the-art TWELVE. But the best of seven series ended four to one for Dennis Conner. Although the number of challengers vying for yachting's ultimate trophy had increased to four that year, the defenders prevailed again. It seemed that, after 24 unsuccessful challenges, the America's Cup was anchored permanently at the New York Yacht Club.
FREEDOM, sailing downwind to victory in 1980
(two overleaf, left).

The Cup match of 1983, between challenger AUSTRALIA II and defender LIBERTY, was a cliff-hanger. Each yacht scored three wins. In the deciding seventh race, skipper John Bertrand of AUSTRALIA II found better air on the downwind leg and rounded the mark with a narrow lead. On the final windward leg he covered Conner's LIBERTY in a duel of 47 tacks and helmed AUSTRALIA II across the finish line to take the gun. An incredible winning streak was finally broken.
AUSTRALIA II, reaching for the America's Cup with spinnaker and a gossamer staysail (two overleaf, right).

The medicine prescribed against boredom by the "Freemantle Doctor" for sailors participating in the 1987 America's Cup competition on Gage Road off Freemantle, Western Australia, was a brisk 20 to 30-knot southwesterly breeze. Administered daily at about noon, it was quite effective and would provide some welcome excitement for spectators of the 1987 Cup competition in the Indian Ocean off Western Australia. It would also put the seventeen 12-Meter yachts and their crews to a severe test.

Two of the six contenders for the defence dropped out early, leaving four Twelves to battle it out for the honour of keeping the America's Cup in the trophy room of the Royal Perth Yacht Club.

In 1983, Alan Bond's AUSTRALIA II had been the first challenger to win the America's Cup. In 1987, Bond makes a bid for the defence with AUSTRALIA IV.
Her opponent in this elimination race is Kevin Parry's KOOKABURRA II, also sailing for the the Royal Perth Yacht Club. As they approach the upwind mark on the first weather leg AUSTRALIA IV, on starboard, crosses the bow of KOOKABURRA II (opposite, top).

After a gybeing duel in the downwind stretch, KOOKABURRA II manages to break through AUSTRALIA IV's cover and take the lead (opposite, bottom).

At a distance only her sail number, KA 15, distinguishes KOOKABURRA III from her almost identical, but slightly older sister and rival KOOKABURRA II. Convincingly besting her three opponents in all elimination rounds earned KOOKABURRA III, skippered by Ian Murray, the right to defend the Cup (above, left).

STEAK & KIDNEY, of the Eastern Australian Defence Syndicate, hailed from the Royal Sydney Yacht Club. Seen here reaching under spinnaker, she was the fourth contender for the defence, but never posed a serious threat to her three rivals from Western Australia (above, right).

An unprecedented number of 13 Twelves from six countries arrived at Freemantle to vie for the challenge. Six hailed from the United States. Both France and Italy had sent two yachts, while Canada, England and New Zealand were competing with one boat each. The aging COURAGEOUS, obviously no longer competitive against her 12 younger state-of-the-art sisters, withdrew. After three round robins, in which each yacht had to match race her 11 rivals once, the four highest scorers met in the semi-finals. The first yacht to win four races in that series would be the challenger.

ITALIA of the Yacht Club Italiano in Genoa displays the colours of her country. Helmed by Aldo Migliaccio she finished seventh (opposite, top left).

CHALLENGE FRANCE of Marseille lacked boat speed. Skippered by Yves Pajot she only scored a few points and came in a disappointing last (opposite, top right).

The yacht USA represented the Saint Francis Yacht Club of San Francisco and placed sixth under skipper Tom Blackaller and helmsman Paul Cayard (opposite, bottom left).

AZZURRA from the Yacht Club Costa Smeralda in Porto Cervo on the Italian island of Sardinia, beam reaching under a gossamer spinnaker with Mauro Pelaschier at the helm. She placed 11th (opposite, bottom right).

EAGLE, of the Newport Harbour Yacht Club in California displays her bold graphics as she beats to windward. She ended up in tenth position under skipper Rod Davis (above, left).

John Kolius skippered AMERICA II of the New York Yacht Club to the semi-finals. One of her crew, halfway up the mast to untangle a fouled line, casts his shadow into the mainsail (above, right).

A locking mechanism at the masthead of a 12-Meter yacht makes it impossible to reef her 1,200 square foot mainsail. This means that in high winds the yacht is "overpowered"; she carries too much sail. The combination of shifty gusts exceeding 35 knots and the typical steep seas of Gage Road caused tense situations for contestants and provided dazzling scenes for spectators.

Her wake, almost at right angles to her downwind course, is clear evidence that CRUSADER has just recovered from a severe broach to port, which even a helmsman as experienced as Harold Cudmore was unable to prevent (opposite).

Responding to the wind shift, CRUSADER has now gybed her mainsail. Another shift in the wind brings her close to a starboard broach. At this point the bowman tries to dip the forward end of the spinnaker pole under the forestay to complete the spinnaker gybe. The strong wind keeps the spinnaker full. Flying free, it casts a stark shadow on the glittering sea (above, left).

She is back on her feet again, but now her stem slams into a wave that sweeps across her entire foredeck and all but buries the bowman. The strong breeze keeps the spinnaker full, although it is still flying free (above, right).

CRUSADER of the Royal Thames Yacht Club of London finished in fifth position.

More drama unfolds on the challengers' course as the wind reaches a velocity that takes competition right to the limit ....

FRENCH KISS, in the foreground, has just gybed her mainsail and the bowman is dipping her spinnaker pole. But she has sailed beyond the mark, visible on the right of her spinnaker. HEART OF AMERICA, seeing a chance to gain an advantage by cutting to the inside, is about to gybe her mainsail. The spinnakers of both yachts are flying free, without the spinnaker pole attached to the guy (opposite).

HEART OF AMERICA has just gybed her mainsail when the spinnaker is hit by a strong gust and explodes (above, left).

Trying to hold her position, HEART OF AMERICA attempts to hoist a new spinnaker. But another burst of wind breaks the spinnaker stops before the hoist can be completed. The untrimmed spinnaker fills and slams the spinnaker pole aganst the forestay with a force that puts an angle bend into it. Adding to this calamity, a tangled line snares the bowman and yanks him off the foredeck.

Being dragged through the water on the yacht's starboard side, he manages to hang on to the spinnaker sheet until he is picked up by a rescue boat (above, right).

HEART OF AMERICA, sailing for the Chicago Yacht Club and skippered by Buddy Melges, had to retire from this race. She finished the round robin series in ninth place.

With high plumes of spray shooting from her bow and leaving a boiling wake, FRENCH KISS of the Societé Nautique de Sète gives a magnificent display of "sailing on the edge" as she flies downwind. Helmed by Marc Pajot, the French yacht reached the semi-finals (overleaf, left).

CANADA II of the Royal Nova Scotia Yacht Squadron was designed by Bruce Kirby of Laser fame. Capable of good speed on reaches and runs, she is seen here beating upwind, which was not her strong point. Skippered by Laser world champion Terry Neilson, CANADA II finished in eighth position (overleaf, right).

NEW ZEALAND, designed by Bruce Farr, Ron Holland and Bruce Davidson, was the first Twelve constructed of fibreglass. After her stunning performance of 34 wins and only five losses in three round robins, "Kiwi Magic" was considered the most formidable contender for the challenge. But in the semi-finals her young skipper Chris Dickson had to yield to veteran Dennis Conner, whose STARS & STRIPES was the first yacht to score four wins. This earned STARS & STRIPES the right to challenge the Cup defender, KOOKABURRA III.

NEW ZEALAND, dubbed "Kiwi Magic", in a burst of speed under spinnaker on a broad reach (below).

A close-up of "Kiwi Magic" shows details of deck layout and the on-board computer display mounted on the mast under the gooseneck (above).

In an astounding comeback, Dennis Conner's STARS & STRIPES of the San Diego Yacht Club defeated KOOKABURRA III in a clean sweep of four straight wins to recapture the America's Cup for the United States (opposite).

Tacking, KOOKABURRA crashes into a wave that erupts in a burst of spray. This time the bowman, who usually has to bear the brunt in rough seas, is spared (overleaf).

WINDSURFING

In less than three decades windsurfing has catapulted from relative obscurity into a success story that now is legend.

From Italy's Lake Garda to Indian Ocean beaches, from the Baltic Sea to British Columbia, millions became addicted to this exciting new form of sailing. Windsurfing made its Olympic debut in 1984. The Bering Strait, the English Channel and even the Atlantic have been conquered on a windsurfer.

The windsurfer is not only the most agile, but also the fastest craft under sail. As technology advanced, new speed records were set year after year. In 1996 the Hobie Trifoiler, a multihull capable of skimming over the water on wings like a hydrofoil, managed to establish a marginal edge over the swift board by clocking 44.55 knots. But it was a short lived triumph. Just a few months later, the Australian Simon McKeon toppled the Trifoiler's record by hurling his windsurfer over the official distance of 500 meters at an astounding speed of 46.52 knots or 86.15 kilometers per hour.

However, soon after the initial concept of windsurfing had caught on, this new sport was to experience an entirely different dimension. A group of Hawaiians at Kailua Bay on the east coast of Oahu, among them school teacher Rick Naish, whose son Robby would later dominate the sport for years, realised that the great surf of the islands offered a unique chance to combine boardsailing with surfing. After all, surfing originated in Hawaii and had been the popular pastime of native islanders for centuries. Experimenting with different board shapes and sails, the Kailua group developed rigs better suited to utilize the combined forces of strong trade wind and high wave. Gradually this would lead to a unique style, distinctly different from flat water windsurfing and course racing. Daring jumps and turns combined into a bewildering array of spectacular maneuvers.

Fascinated by photographs and stories in magazines, enthusiastic windsurfing afficionados flocked to the islands from all corners of the world. It would take these newcomers a fair bit of time to catch up to their Hawaiian role models. But dedication and perseverance paid off, and eventually the most talented managed to break into the ranks of experts. Meanwhile, ongoing improvements of windsurfer equipment made stunts like the 360 degree loop, considered impossible not too long ago, part of the routine performance of many accomplished windsurfers. Today even double loops are no longer uncommon.

Since the early 1980s, international wave competitions have been organised wherever conditions are favourable, including Australia, France, Germany, the Caribbean and Japan. In Holland a contest at Zandfoort beach drew 100,000 spectators – a record number for any sporting event ever held in that country. But no place on earth can rival sun-drenched Hawaii, where an intensely blue Pacific breaks into white crested surf on its palm fringed beaches.

Two components are vital for a wave contest: surf and a sideshore breeze. Strong surf – often with high wave faces – forms when the ever-present ocean swell runs into an obstacle like a rapidly shoaling coast. A good sideshore breeze is usually found in an area where the topography accelerates the prevailing wind and deflects it to follow the contours of the shoreline. In Hawaii, the beaches of Diamond Head on Oahu and Hookipa on Maui are considered the world's best. They are the choice sites for wave competitions. When wind and surf are up, dozens of windsurfers can be seen here, honing their skills or just having fun any day of the week.

At Diamond Head waves are generally not as high as at Hookipa and the surf runs into the beach with a gentler rumble. This permits slalom racing, a contest sailed on a figure-eight course. One buoy is set close inshore and a second one in the deeper water just outside the breaking surf. After a running "Le Mans" start from the beach, up to eight competitors have to round both marks twice. Several elimination heats determine the finalists. The first sailor to reach the beach in the concluding race is declared the champion. Fast boards are used in slalom, a favourite with spectators, because the exciting gybe mark roundings and close finishes are easy to follow. Hookipa does not allow slalom racing; the surf often breaks right onto a beach strewn with barely submerged rocks.

Wave competitions are held at both locations and require superior skills, particularly at Hookipa, where conditions are usually more demanding and wave faces frequently reach a height of 20 feet. In a race against the clock, competitors are allowed only eight minutes to perform as many maneuvers as possible. Choosing the right waves for jumps, transitions and surfing is critical. Moves like forward and backward loops, windmills, distance jumps, table top jumps, off-the-lip jumps, top turns, bottom turns and others are scrutinized by the critical eyes of five judges. The more daring, innovative and varied the performance, the higher the score. In wave competition two contestants meet one-on-one in heats during the elimination rounds, with the winner advancing to the next heat. These eliminations continue until the final two competitors battle it out for the championship.

The seemingly elegant ease with which today's masters of Diamond Head and Hookipa execute their stunning repertoire of breathtaking jumps, loops and turns is sheer poetry in motion.

In the early years of wave performance, larger boards and longer booms did not allow the spectacular maneuvers in high surf and strong winds that are common today.
A competitor "milks" a wave right into the shore to add points to his score in non-typically moderate conditions at Hookipa (preceding pages).

Using the waves at Diamond Head as a ramp, the first jumps were attempted and successfully landed (above).

Gradually, equipment improved and skills progressed. This made sailing in more demanding conditions possible.

A strong wind at Hookipa provides enough power for Peter Cabrinha to force his board through a shore break that is too soft for a jump (opposite).

Once outside the surf, he finds a suitable wave to carve a top turn. The high arc of white spray flying off his board underscores this stunning maneuver. Peter Cabrinha, known for his elegant style, was one of the first Hawaiian wave aces (overleaf).

Nature has chosen the breaking surf to reveal her inexhaustible palette of blues and greens. The camera can only capture a split second of the ever changing splendour of colours and shapes.

The strong sideshore breeze tears feathers from the crest of this "mast high" wave at Hookipa. A sailboard accentuates the surf as it changes from the deep blue-green of solid wave to shades of translucent blue and spills out in a pool of white foam (opposite).

Stuart Sawyer of England takes to the air at Diamond Head not more than 10 feet from my lens (above).

Hookipa on the island of Maui faces north and is directly exposed to the open Pacific. Ocean swells running into the abruptly shoaling beach often create a strong surf with a steep wave face. Combined with an easterly wind that is accelerated by the topography of Maui, this results in conditions that demand the utmost in skill and experience.

Outrunning the wave that tries to catch up to him as it breaks in an unruly pattern of aquamarine and white, this windsurfer makes it safely to the shore (overleaf).

Slalom is the spectators' favourite, because exciting gybe mark roundings and close finishes are easy to follow.

Women's slalom at Diamond Head. After the first inshore turn Jill Boyer is in the lead of this elimination round (opposite, top).

But in the final run to shore Lena Kerr wins this heat and advances to the next round (opposite, bottom).

A wave contest is a race against the clock. Competitors have eight minutes to perform as many maneuvers as possible. Jutta Müller of Germany gybes her board inshore and heads out again, hoping to catch another good wave and improve her score (above).

Sonja Evenson, a native of Norway, took up residence in Hawaii. She achieved her goal of being the first European woman to win a wave competition at Diamond Head in 1985 (right).

US 1111 is the sail number identifying champion Robby. Here he executes a perfect loop at Diamond Head (above).

Winning his first World Championship at age 13, Robby Naish reigned supreme for over a decade. By 1989 he had garnered 11 World Titles (right).

Robby Naish is first around the inshore mark in this elimination round of the men's slalom of 1985 at Diamond Head. Robert Terriitehau of New Caledonia is in second place and Richard Why of Hawaii is third (opposite, top).

Close racing in the "washing machine", the surf of a collapsing wave. Seasoned windsurfers traverse this foaming obstacle with ea (opposite, bottom).

When photographing in the water there is no chance escaping the washing machine. Camera clutched to my chest, I must endure the indignity of being tumbled like a cork as the surf sweeps inshore and literally spits me out onto the beach.

In the final round, Robby Naish prevails against two other Hawaiian competitors, Maui Meyer and Peter Cabrinha, who com in second and third (overleaf).

An "off the lip" jump is a difficult maneuver, because the wave keeps moving inshore as the windsurfer takes to the air from its crest. The trick is to catch the "lip" of a suitable wave to take off from and to land on the same wave again by giving the board a shoreward twist when in the air.

Although this wave is quite unruly, it poses no problem for a contestant as experienced as Richard Whyte (opposite, top).

His board leaves a delicate trail in the transparent wave to the point where this competitor takes off from the crest for his "off the lip" jump (opposite, centre).

A combination of top turn, bottom turn and off the lip jump gives Robby Naish the highest score (opposite, bottom).

Peter Cabrinha's "table top" jump should bring him good points (above).

Keoni Lucas of Hawaii seems to be suspended in the air momentarily as he gets in a perfect "off the lip" jump at Hookipa, while Hidemi Furuyo of Japan surfs down the face of the following wave (overleaf).

A fair-sized, but smooth wave to serve as a ramp and a strong sideshore wind to provide the power are essential for a high jump. Raphael Salles of France has found both to project him into this spectacular flight at Diamond Head during the 1986 wave contest. In extreme wind conditions jumps as high as 35 feet have been safely landed (two pages overleaf).

Handling a camera in the gentle swell outside the breaking surf is easy. To catch a jumping windsurfer on film is not, because the wave he is going to use as a ramp for his jump conceals his approach and he becomes visible only as he takes to the air. Conversely, photographing a jumper from inside the surf permits following his approach until he takes off, but here the turbulence of the surrounding waves makes it difficult to keep the camera steady enough for a frame-filling shot. Either technique depends largely on patience and luck.

How deep is the ocean, how high is the sky ....
(opposite, top).

These two competitors have approached the same wave from
opposite directions with different intentions. It seems that the board
of the jumper almost touches the tip of the mast of his rival, who
has just completed a top turn. But my 500mm lens exaggerates the
action by compressing the lateral distance that separates the two
daredevils. The flying acrobat is actually about 10 feet further
away. Nonetheless, this picture demonstrates the precision with
which these experts control their boards (opposite, bottom).

Dana Dawes of Hawaii, a top competitor in wave contest and
slalom for years, reigned again at Hookipa in 1990 (right).

Conditions can change quickly at Hookipa. One morning, during a
wave contest, a 25-knot wind tears sheets of spume from an unruly
surf that is not ideal for spectacular maneuvers. Cesare Cesario of
Italy has prudently chosen a smaller sail to stay in control (above).

Only two hours later, the wind has dropped to 15 knots, allowing
World Champion Anders Bringdal of Sweden to use a full-size sail
to display his style by carving a radical top turn that sends a
sparkling semicircle of spray high into the air (overleaf).

SEASONS OF A BAY

The first signs are subtle, barely noticeable. Towards the east, stars surrender their sparkle to a faint blush. Dawn slowly pulls away the cover of night, gently ushering in the morning with a soft hue of amber. A gossamer mist rises silently. Motionless, SAGA floats on a cushion of suspended time.

A thin veil of cloud diffuses the early sunlight to a pale gold that spreads across the liquid expanse. The mood blends perfectly with the aroma of freshly brewed coffee wafting from the cabin.

A flight of geese makes a pass, low over the water. The effortless grace of beating wings is duplicated in the mirrorlike surface of the lake. So delicate is the stillness that a mere whisper of air stirs up a small ruffle, here and there. Cat's paws, heralds of a breeze. Ripples appear, branch out like ribs of an oriental fan, connect into widening patterns. It is time to haul up the anchor. Sails catch the first wind of the day. Slowly the little ship gets under way, leaving behind a softly murmuring trail. She is not in a hurry. It is early yet.

The sun arches higher and the breeze freshens. Soft ripples grow into waves; valleys and hills of cobalt blue, crowned by transparent, turquoise ridges. Now the yacht comes to life; eagerly she rushes ahead. Gleaming white plumes leap from her bow as she attacks wave after wave.

By mid-afternoon, a towering bank of ominous clouds appears in the south. Moving rapidly, it covers the sky within minutes. Furious gusts rattle the rigging, tear at sails already reefed in anticipation of the squall. Jagged flashes of lightning pierce the dark gloom. Crashing thunder competes with the howling wind. Suddenly we are surrounded by an eerie calm. The respite is cut short by a deluge so fierce that visibility is down to zero.

The display of nature's temper is short-lived. As the downpour moderates, a large yacht heaves into sight. The squall has caught her by surprise and twisted her spinnaker around the forestay into an hourglass. It is still raining hard, but astern a band of glittering silver on the lake marks the trailing edge of the squall clouds. Before long the sky is swept clear. Our spinnaker, set to a following wind, fills and displays its billowing glory.

Gradually the sun abdicates its brightness, until it burns like a disc of fire. The breeze softens and our speed drops considerably. Entering the bay, we glide past a brigantine, silhouetted against an evening sky aglow with radiant orange. The noise of an engine would offend this tranquility, so we ghost along. As night falls, we pick up the mooring lines at our club to end a memorable sail across the western lake.

Wind furnishes texture, light provides colour and contrast – water responds, reflects, underscoring the mood. Soft pastels and gentle ripples, tumbling swell and grey doom, glittering crests of translucent blue, the lake's character is unique. The harshest frost of winter cannot pull an icy blanket over its deep waters. Even a sweltering hot spell at the height of summer will raise its temperature barely enough for a short, invigorating dip. The seasons are pronounced, the variety of settings is infinite. The sailing yacht adds the final accent to this ever-changing magic.

The photographs on the following pages were taken during the sailing season on a stretch of water extending some five miles to the southwest of Toronto, the fair city on Lake Ontario I now call home. It is known as Humber Bay.

On weekends, yachts of 15 clubs in the Toronto area participate in regattas. During spring and fall, winds are usually stronger and more reliable than in the summer.

Dr. Colin Baxter's Two-Tonner MARAUDER of the National Yacht Club shows off her colourful flying sails in the first race of the season (preceding pages).

Chris Steer's C&C 34 MAGGIE KELLY of the Royal Canadian Yacht Club has a good lead in this 35-mile offshore spring race. (opposite, top).

The annual racing schedule includes a number of overnight offshore races which start in Toronto on Friday nights. The triangular courses lead to shipping bouys at the western and southern shores of Lake Ontario and cover about 65 nautical miles.
Start of an "overnighter" (opposite, bottom)

During the summer it is not uncommon for the sea breeze to be lifted by a flow of warm air from the land miles before it reaches the shore. This results in light and fickle wind conditions that require concentration to keep spinnakers flying (above).

Summer haze seems to blend the horizon into the lake. A whisper of wind barely holds up the spinnaker which reflects in the gently rippled surface of the water (right).

Even at the height of summer a fresh easterly or westerly wind can prevail for several days.

MOONRAKER thrives in the brisk breeze that makes her the MORC North American Champion of 1984 (opposite).

During that same championship, one of her competitors is out of control momentarily, when a sudden shift in the wind puts her lee rail under in an extreme broach (above).

Sustained strong southerlies can produce conditions that are somewhat less than ideal. Seas running north crash headlong into the breakwater of the horseshoe-shaped bay and are thrown back to form fairly high and unruly waves. These circumstances prevailed in the 1977 North American Half-Ton Championship.

ELAN II sails in the trough of a wave that completely eclipses the Toronto shoreline (right).

For TRIOMPHE II, the consequences were more dramatic. The combination of high waves and a 30-knot wind brought down her mast (overleaf).

Sails catch the first wind of the day .....
As we get under way, a thin veil of cloud diffuses the early sun to a pale gold that spreads across the liquid expanse. The mood blends perfectly with the aroma of freshly brewed coffee wafting from the cabin (opposite, top left).

The sudden squall has surprised this yacht and twisted her spinnaker around the forestay into an hourglass (opposite, top right).

A band of glittering silver on the lake marks the trailing edge of the squall clouds. Our spinnaker, set to a following wind, fills and we are on course again (opposite, bottom left).

Entering the bay, we glide past a brigantine, silhouetted against an evening sky aglow with radiant orange. As night falls, we pick up the mooring lines at our club to end an exhilarating sail across the western lake (opposite, bottom right).

Five-year-old Cynthia Baker of the Boulevard Club handles her Optimist with confidence and poise (above).

Exuberance reflects in Magnus Clarke's face as the ten-year-old of the Royal Canadian Yacht Club is about to win his Optimist race (right).

As early as October a brisk breeze can put a nip in the air. Even at midday, the sun's lower angle produces acute colours and detail.

Blustery fall winds under a clear blue sky send these IOR I racers off on a lively spinnaker reach.
AMAZING GRACE, Robert Herron's custom C&C 44 of the Port Credit Yacht Club leads Gerry Moog's 45-foot custom Frers DYNAMO of the Royal Canadian Yacht Club (above).

ABISHAG heads for shelter to escape a thunderstorm (left).

BONAVENTURE, a 53 foot custom C&C owned by B. Herman of the Island Yacht Club, sailing hard on the wind (opposite, top).

SHARKS are the most numerous keelboat class in Canada. Over 2,000 of these affordable 24-footers sail in North America and Europe.
Peter Vickery's ZUCCHINI, Shark Class World Champion of 1989, leads in a Boulevard Club race (opposite, bottom).

A fitting backdrop for the final race of the season – the gilded skyline of Toronto (overleaf).

AT ANCHOR

The sailing ship lives off the wind. Her ability to harness the breeze and achieve an equilibrium of motion and stability is like an act of sorcery that seemingly defies the laws of physics. Nimbly, she captures the light and fickle zephyr, responds to the freshening breeze with quickened pace and jaunty slant. But when the wind really brings the sea to life, crowns toppling wave with gleaming white crest, only then can the sailing ship's spirited aspirations be fulfilled. Taking up the gauntlet, she rides the wind. Adapting her rhythm to the rhythm of the sea, she sweeps along with a purposeful grace. When sailing on the edge, her performance is a fascinating display of power and poise. It is a sight that has inspired painters and poets for centuries.

Intent on capturing the old-worldly essence of the sail, but woefully short of talent for pen or brush, I resorted to a modern tool: the camera.

The most expedient way to take up the chase is from a light aircraft. Flying allows a good overview of the racing fleet. Individual yachts can be targeted and "buzzed" on low passes. As an ex-pilot I have no problem communicating with other pilots. Competent and accommodating, they are often willing to remove the door on the photographer's side of the aircraft to make camera panning easier. A hovering helicopter is easier to shoot from, but quite expensive. I have used helicopters only at the America's Cup in Freemantle, where light aircraft were not permitted to fly below 800 feet in the area of the race courses.

Aerial photographs are quite effective, but the bird's eye view has limits. A power boat not only offers a different perspective, it provides the low camera angle essential for capturing the intimate relationship between yacht and sea.

Why drivers of the power boats I hired turned out to be inconsiderate speed jockeys will forever remain a conundrum to me. Accelerating and throttling back suddenly, or spinning the boat around without warning, they seemed determined to foil my efforts and put my equipment at risk. This was frustrating enough in any event. When conditions were good, however, missing out on excellent opportunities, only because of the driver's erratic behaviour, would aggravate me to no end. I suspected being the victim of a conspiracy, until I compared notes with other photographers. Learning that they fared no better was consoling, but hardly a solution. Driving a boat myself was the alternative.

Operating a power boat and photographing is not as difficult as one might imagine; even in rough weather it is my preferred modus operandi. Most of the SORC pictures shown here, including the bow-on photograph of BOOM BOOM, as well as the other double page pictures and those of the Southern Cross Cup and the Sydney-Hobart race were taken that way. When taking frontal shots in a strong breeze the trick is to keep slightly to the leeward side of the yacht .   If she looses her footing in a sudden gust, a yacht will round up to windward.

Large, official press boats available at the America's Cup are crowded to capacity with accredited writers and photographers. Named HELLCAT or DIVER, they are indeed the floating torture chambers their names imply. They are the only boats permitted close to the race course, but not close enough. Once I sneaked out by myself in a low 15-foot Whaler. I was careful not to interfere with the racing and had already taken some good close-ups of COURAGEOUS when the Coast Guard spotted my little boat and ordered me back to port with a severe warning.

Disrespect for the rules of nature can have more serious consequences. At the start of the 1979 Ocean Triangle race at Miami I had captured several yachts fighting hard to keep their spinnakers flying in a gusty 15-knot northerly. Caught up in the excitement, I pursued the fleet in a rented 20-foot Shamrock some ten miles into the Gulf Stream. Halfway back to port the Shamrock's propeller shaft broke. Instantly, the disabled boat began to drift north at a steady rate; we were at the mercy of the Gulf Stream. There was no radio aboard, not an ounce of food nor a drop of water. No other vessel was within hailing range. And the wind was building.

Three days later, the Shamrock was sighted by a trawler, 125 miles north of Miami, 25 miles out to sea, well past the shipping lanes of the North West Channel and the island of Grand Bahama. A line snaked through the air, with great care I secured it to the Shamrock's bow cleat. During the five hour long tow to Fort Pierce, my gaze kept returning to the sturdy trawler's stern, just to assure myself that I wasn't hallucinating again.

The first night had been a terrifying experience. The northerly increased to gale force. Steep 15-foot seas, with spume tearing off breaking crests, slammed into the helpless craft and threatened to capsize it. A northbound freighter ploughed by so close that its bow wave swamped the cockpit. I bailed for my life to keep the boat afloat.

By midmorning the wind abated, but the calm of a devastatingly empty sea was worse than the stormy trial: waiting for the verdict – guilty or not guilty to the charge of being reckless. The jury stayed out for two long, lonely, doubt-filled days. Finally, the sentence: Guilty as charged – released on probation.

Back in Miami, I learned that eight yachts had been forced to abandon the Ocean Triangle race that first night because of serious gear failure. PIRANA had lost a crew overboard shortly after rounding Great Isaac Light. Extended efforts by the yacht and the Coast Guard to find him in the turbulent seas had been unsuccessful.

A week later I went on a sailing trip from Miami to Nassau in the Bahamas. The pilot chart for the islands contained the following description of the Gulf Stream: *Its volume is far greater than the waters poured into the oceans by all the great rivers of the world combined. It passes through the Florida Straits at a velocity of up to five miles per hour. Wave height and steepness in a northerly wind will increase 25 per cent above normal.* Indeed!

For the 1981 SORC I had trailered a 19-foot Boston Whaler from Toronto to Florida, expecting a cornucopia of good photographs for my effort. But the first five races yielded only windward pictures. The one exception was a spinnaker shot in the Miami – Nassau race, taken very late in the afternoon and probably underexposed. Disappointed and frustrated, I convinced myself that my luck was bound to change in the final race; the Nassau Cup would not dare deny me spinnakers. I had not planned on taking the Whaler to the Bahamas. To tackle the ocean in an open boat with a low freeboard, to find my way to Nassau, some 170 nautical miles east of Fort Lauderdale, with nothing higher than 80 feet above sea level in between and only a compass to navigate by, was audacious. But the Whaler was fast, had not one, but two brawny 80 HP engines; if one engine conked out, the the other would pull me through. Besides, the route was familiar, I had sailed it twice before.

Even in a moderate sea, crossing the Gulf Stream was a torturous, four hour bronco ride. The Whaler tried its best to toss me overboard as it hurled from wave to wave. Lashed to the steering console I had to stand upright. Blinded by flying spray, unable to read the compass, I had to steer by the sun's reflection on the water, adjusting my bearing every half hour as the sun arched higher and further into the south. Halfway across, some-body fired at me from a barge-like vessel. The bullets whizzed by without finding their target. I had never been shot at before; the experience left my throat very dry. Delayed for five hours in Bimini by Bahama Customs, I spent the most peaceful night of my life anchored in the middle of the Great Bahama Bank, under a canopy of silent stars close enough to touch. Under way again at sunrise, I slipped off the Bank onto the Tongue of the Ocean – from the light ochre of little more than one fathom into the deep blue of a thousand fathoms – and tied up at the Pilot House dock in Nassau harbour at 10.30 AM. I needn't have bothered. The Nassau Cup was a light air "drifter". I saved my film and wrote off the affair as a lesson well learned. But school wasn't over yet. On the return trip, barely 25 miles out of Nassau, the Whaler's port engine gave up its ghost. On one engine, it took five gruelling hours of constant wrestling with the wheel and almost the last drop of fuel to get back to Nassau. I wondered whether fate would have granted me a second reprieve, had the engine died in the Gulf Stream.

Ironically, my bravado performances were in vain. The shot of TENACIOUS, broaching in the 1979 Ocean Triangle race, was taken well before I entered the Gulf Stream. And the 1981 SORC yielded three good windward shots. Even the only spinnaker photograph was better than expected (all five appear as double pages).

Sea lore abounds with sailing vessels possessed of human traits, good or bad. Conrad's BRUTE and Slocum's SPRAY spring readily to mind. Any dyed-in-the-wool sailor will agree that some yachts do have a personality.

SAGA certainly does. She is straining at her lines now, twenty four feet of impatient expectation. The wind has come up, her halyards are tapping out an urgent message on the mast: "Let's not waste that wind". I close my note pad, hoist sails, set her free. The breeze carries her along – a bird on the wing. I scrub the deck, ease off the sheets just a little. Then I sit back and watch her go, fascinated by her uncanny instinct for the wind as she nimbly balances gust and shift to hold her course. The world has changed a lot in the three decades we have been together, SAGA hasn't. After all those years, her way with the wind still fascinates me.

Much goes to SAGA's credit. My sons Richard and Martin have retained the passion for sailing she kindled in them; now their growing families share that ardour. It is doubtful that Margaret would put up with my idiosyncrasies, were it not for the mitigating prospect of weekends on SAGA. Bringing my camera aboard SAGA had unforeseen consquences. When the NONSUCH picture, taken in 1969, brought an unexpected return, I traded business suit for sailing jacket and became a marine photographer. SAGA had arranged my great escape.

SAGA is an unorthodox photo boat; relying on the wind she lacks the speed of a power boat. But she offers a much stabler platform, particularly in strong winds and heavy seas. When I took the shot of TRIOMPHE's mastbreak in a 30-knot southerly, she excelled. Under a reefed mainsail she handled better than any power boat could have. Stalking yachts on Lake Ontario, we log 2,000 to 3,000 nautical miles during a short sailing season. The engine is taboo, the strong breeze is our best friend, helping us to do well in a race occasionally.

Extreme winds are rare on Lake Ontario and I had often wondered how SAGA would stand up to a severe blow. A few years ago I got my answer. Going across the lake from Toronto on a beam reach in a steady 12-knot westerly and under a sunny August sky had been the stuff a Sunday sailors's dream is made of. We were crossing the bar at the wide mouth of the Niagara river when Margaret, with an expression of grave concern on her face, pointed aft. I turned my head; my heart almost missed a beat. In forty five years of sailing I had never seen a sky that foreboding. A boiling mass of graphite black, towering over a narrow, horizontal slab of slate grey, came rushing towards us at an incredible speed. Without a moment's hesitation, we struck the genoa, tied a deep reef into the main and cleared the cockpit of any loose stuff. Unfortunately, there was no time to take a picture of this phenomenal spectacle. Close behind us the lake was jumping in a wild uproar.

Seconds later it hit. As if pushed by a giant's fist, SAGA was planing up a river that was instantly alive with spume. It is difficult to judge speed in such conditions; the speedometer needle rested solidly against the stop at the 15 knot mark. Running before this mighty squall with only a minimum of main up, SAGA sped past the Niagara-on-the-Lake Yacht Club towards Niagara Falls, leaving not a wake, but a high rooster tail behind her. Strangely enough there was neither thunder, lightning nor a drop of rain, only this incredible wind, under racing clouds, howling in the rigging. After running upriver for a while I was concerned that we might end up at the Falls, if this blow should last much longer. Cautiously, I put the helm down. To my amazement, SAGA responded quite well, only the main started to flog madly. Sheeting in halfway quieted down the sail somewhat and SAGA came up fairly close to the wind. Heeled well over, but not taking on water, she moved ahead at four knots. Encouraged, I put the helm down hard. Her foredeck vanished in a blanket of spray, but she put her bow through the wind. To hold our position, we then alternately ran, reached and tacked. Cars on the riverside road stopped, our crazy performance drew an audience.

In less than half an hour it was over. Sailing back to the Yacht Club we had to thread our way through a maze of flotsam on the river. By the time we tied up at the dock and lowered the sail, the wind was down to ten knots. Club members advised us to keep the mooring lines slack. Short as it had been, this squall had pushed up the water level at the yacht club by almost three feet. From the weather report we learned that the wind had peaked at 60 knots. Slowly, our adrenalin rush gave way to a warm feeling of satisfaction. Thankful that she had brought us through this onslaught unscathed, we drank a toast to SAGA, the valiant little ship.

When the first photographs of Hawaiian windsurfers appeared in magazines, I designed a watertight housing for my camera. Reg Wilkins, goldsmith, dedicated underwater photographer and friend, built it for me. As soon as the housing was ready, I flew to Honolulu and flung myself confidently into the surf at Diamond Head. The first ten-foot wave knocked the housing right out of my tightly clenched hands and dragged me tumbling across the shallow reef. Bleeding from several coral cuts, I stumbled ashore and looked back to where the surf was pounding my camera and brand new housing to bits on the submerged rocks of the sea shelf.

But I returned. With advice from windsurfers and a lot of practice I have learned to treat currents and surf with the caution and respect they demand. A new camera housing is securely strapped to my wrist. Fins and a custom made float jacket with variable buoyancy allow me to swim toward the break, dive – surfer style – through the waves and get to the other side of the breaking surf. There I blow air into the jacket for buoyancy and head back into the break, hoping to catch a windsurfer on a wave. The inflated jacket makes shooting easier, but diving into a wave impossible. As the unrelenting surf sweeps inshore it tumbles me around and pushes me along until it fizzles out near the beach. If lucky, I get three or four pictures, one of which might not be spoiled by spray on the lens port. I deflate my jacket and swim out again for another cycle of diving, floating, shooting and tumbling, and another, and another – as long as the windsurfers are out. Photographing windsurfers at Diamond Head is always exhausting and often rewarding. When I come in to reload the camera after an hour of shooting, I feel as if I have swallowed half the Pacific. The waves at Hookipa on Maui have proven too powerful for my in-the-water technique. Shooting windsurfers from the shore with a 500mm lens has produced very satisfactory results.

The adage "a camera doesn't lie" must stem from a time when the range of focal lengths of lenses was limited. Extreme wide angle- or telephoto lenses treat the truth much like a seasoned politician – for maximum effect. A short wide angle lens will stretch the deck of a 30-footer to make it appear like that of a supertanker. The long telephoto lens used at a short distance compacts the same boat to the shape of an oval salad bowl or transforms a crowded mark rounding to a scene of utter chaos from where there is no escape without multiple collisions. I contend that distorting the aesthetic lines of a yacht is a violation of her intrinsic beauty and use these lenses seldom and with prudence.

Sea water spray is corrosive and rust spots will appear within hours if cameras are not cleaned thoroughly and as soon as possible. A professional servicing after each trip has prevented equipment failure so far. But the possibility of a breakdown worries me constantly and I always carry two spare camera bodies. Yachting photography calls for a shoot-and-run approach which favours the compactness of a 35mm camera. Having tested the products of half a dozen top rated manufacturers, I found that the Canon line suits me best. Their lenses are superb and the camera bodies are rugged and lightweight. Canon also offers the best service worldwide.

Occasionally I have tried a free sample of different film manufacturers. So far this has only confirmed my conviction that Kodachrome is outstanding.

Traditionally, yachting has been the domain of men. Perhaps that is why a ship always has been – and still is – referred to as "she". In days of old it was even considered bad luck to have a woman aboard. Today the all-male crew is the exception, and for a good reason: women have proven to be every bit as skilled and competitive, and have sea legs just as steady as those of men. Women have shown their mettle on square-riggers, keel boats, in dinghies and on windsurfers. Single-handing their yachts, women have circled the globe. MAIDEN entered and finished the 1989 Whitbread Round-the-World race with an all-female crew. Others have followed. And the "Mermaids" of MIGHTY MARY, with only a male tactician aboard, caused some concern among their all-male rivals by racking up a respectable number of wins in the US defender trials for the 1995 America's Cup.

If I have referred to the sailor as a "he" elsewhere in this book it should be read as to include all women who participate in this exciting sport.

Each time I return from abroad, sun-tanned, my friends call me a lucky devil. In fact, I do consider myself fortunate, because my work is a constant challenge, very exciting and has taken me to far-off places. But travel is not exactly first class. By the time I have packed my photo equipment, an assortment of tools and other useful gadgets, foul weather gear, sailing boots, jeans, pullovers and drip-dry shirts, there is no room left for jacket and tie. I have slept on boats, couches, floors, beaches and in armchairs, cars and vans more often than in hotels. On several occasions I have spent a whole week in a Rent-a-Wreck on the island of Maui, because that would guarantee me a choice spot for windsurfing shots on a crowded roadside overlooking Hookipa beach. Results count. A strong commitment is essential, as is the approval of Aeolus, the god who commands the winds. Travelling thousands of miles to a regatta series that turns out to be a "drifter" is totally frustrating.

There are rewards: sailing on TICONDEROGA, AMERICA and BLUENOSE was to experience the grace and power of true paragons of the sea, a thrill I will not forget for the rest of my life. Meeting the experts of sailing – from windsurfing champions to Tall Ship captains – and listening to their yarns has broadened my understanding of the sport considerably. Interviews with Ted Turner and Paul Elvström were revelations of different mental and pragmatic approaches to winning yacht races from two of the most successful sailors of our time. But the greatest reward is to see in my viewfinder a yacht, every stitch of canvas set and straining to the breeze in sensuous curves, leaving behind her a white foaming trail as she heads for the turning mark in a race or shapes her course to a port on another continent.

In a pinch a helping hand was seldom far away. Late one Christmas Eve, the owner a jewellery shop in Sydney's fashionable Double Bay replaced the bent coupling ring of a lens I would need for the start of the Sydney-Hobart race on Boxing Day. A mechanic in Waikiki freed a jammed leg of my tripod with his pipe wrench. None other than Sir James Hardy, the Australian 12-Meter skipper, took me to the hospital in Newport, Rhode Island to have a nasty cut in my leg repaired. Nicknamed "Gentleman Jim" by the Aussie squad, he watched me being stitched up and shrugged off my thanks with this pragmatic observation: "Don't worry, Franz. It might be handy to know where the hospital is, just in case one of our blokes needs attention". The list of those who helped me when trouble arose includes people from all walks of life, truck drivers and yacht owners – total strangers and close friends. All have contributed to this book. I am indebted to Margaret Jacot for her encouragement and the flattering author's portrait, to Jivko Dinev for the line drawings on the inside covers and to Andre Calla, Mike Catalfamo, Magnus Clarke and Cliff Newman for their valuable advice. And last, but certainly not least, I must mention my good friends Peter Vickery and Hans Fogh. Peter designed and made the heavy duty hardware and fittings that have kept my little ship and me going when we were out on the lake in adverse conditions. Hans is the sailor extraordinaire, whose achievements include four world championships in the FLYING DUTCHMAN and SOLING, two Olympic medals, plus a list of national and international titles too long to mention. His advice on sailing matters and contacts abroad have been invaluable.

The production of this book – colour separation, printing and binding – was handled expertly by the Friesen Corporation. Thanks to Bob Hamilton and Mike Fehr, I have gained a little insight into a daunting process.

Coming full circle, I cap the last page by referring to the first page and express my gratitude to Doug Hunter for his complimentary foreword. Regarding the generous advice Doug gives in the final paragraph I would like to offer this caveat: observing the rhythm of a yacht as she interacts with the sea or anticipating a scenario on the race course is a shooting technique I have used whenever possible. But frequently a photograph was the result of spontaneous reaction, which precluded any artistic consideration. The following calculation, an afterthought, was surprising: the 158 pictures in this book were exposed at an average shutter speed of 1/500 second; i.e. the total exposure time for all pictures was less than one third of one second. This would be art in the fast lane.

If my photographs are able to impart to the viewer some of the excitement I felt when taking them, then this book has served its purpose.

Franz Rosenbaum